Girl Online

Girl Online

A User Manual

Joanna Walsh

London • New York

First published by Verso 2022

1 3 5 7 9 10 8 6 4 2

Verso
UK: 6 Meard Street, London W1F 0EG
US: 388 Atlantic Avenue, Brooklyn, NY 11217
versobooks.com

Verso is the imprint of New Left Books

ISBN-13: 978-1-83976-535-3
ISBN-13: 978-1-83976-537-7 (UK EBK)
ISBN-13: 978-1-83976-538-4 (US EBK)

British Library Cataloguing in Publication Data
A catalogue record for this book is available from the British Library

Library of Congress Cataloging-in-Publication Data

Names: Walsh, Joanna, author.
Title: Girl online : a user manual / Joanna Walsh.
Description: First Edition Hardback. | Brooklyn, NY : Verso, 2022. | Includes bibliographical references.
Identifiers: LCCN 2021061656 (print) | LCCN 2021061657 (ebook) | ISBN 9781839765353 (Hardback) | ISBN 9781839765384 (eBook)
Subjects: LCSH: Women—Identity. | Online identities. | Identity (Psychology) | Technology—Social aspects.
Classification: LCC HQ1206 .W233 2022 (print) | LCC HQ1206 (ebook) | DDC 303.48/3082—dc23/eng/20220125
LC record available at https://lccn.loc.gov/2021061656
LC ebook record available at https://lccn.loc.gov/2021061657

Typeset in Sabon by Hewer Text UK Ltd, Edinburgh
Printed and bound by CPI Group (UK) Ltd, Croydon CR0 4YY

There are no girls on the internet.

'The Rules of the Internet', Usenet, c. early 2000s

How to read this book

This book is a user manual.
This book is a virtual manifesto for manual workers.
This book is a work of literary criticism.
This book is a forum post.
This book is a memoir of motherhood.
This book is a historical novel about the internet in the 2000s.
This book is a work of feminist autotheory.
This book is a blog.
This book is a thought experiment.
This book is chick lit.
This book is a piece of code.

To read this book ideally, it is necessary to read all the words in it simultaneously. To read this book, it is necessary to hyperlink. The ideal reader of this book is the internet.

Contents

How to read this book vi

Thought Experiment #1: Switch 1
1. SCREEN GOODS 4

PART I: WOMAN WORKING IN FRONT OF A SCREEN / ALICE UNDERGROUND

Thought Experiment #2: Function 19
2. RELATIVITY 22
Thought Experiment #3: Or 35
3. WORK 37
Thought Experiment #4: Use 54
4. NOT WORKING 57
Thought Experiment #5: Work 66
5. AM I THOSE NAMES 69

PART II: GIRL ONLINE / ALICE THROUGH THE LOOKING GLASS

6. GIRL ONLINE 77
Thought Experiment #6: Sound 110
7. THE UNWRITTEN 113
Thought Experiment #7: Nothing 122

PART III: A USER MANUAL FOR ALICIAN SUBJECTS

8. 'NOW WOULD BE GOOD' 127
Thought Experiment #8: Test 130
9. ALICE ONLINE 132
10. POST-GIRL MANIFESTO 138
Thought Experiment #9: Experimental Evidence of Massive-Scale Emotional Contagion through Social Networks 142

Acknowledgements 143
Notes 145

Thought Experiment #1: Switch

I hope you understand what thinking in chorus means—
for I must confess that I don't.
—Lewis Carroll, *Through the Looking-Glass*

Functionalists hold that mental states are defined by the causal role they play in a system.[1] *In the Chinese Nation thought experiment, pain is a point in time. It occurs when enough components say it does.*

Say there's a woman working alone in a room at a screen and the screen screens her privacy—the privacy she also is. She is sitting in front of logic gates that have not yet closed behind her. Let's say this logic gate is a pain switch.

In programming, a logic gate has a single binary function. From a dual input it produces a single output. It does this by way of conjunctions, like AND, which has the symbol '∧', or OR, which has the symbol '∨'—which is a non-exclusive or—and XOR, which is an exclusive or, where only one thing is true, or the other. This switch's XOR logic gate is PAIN/NOTPAIN. The pain is not any specific sort, physical or mental; it is the pain the woman is feeling. Any sort of pain may go through the gate so long as she is willing to call it pain.

Say there are enough women sitting alone, each in a room, each in front of a logic gate. Say their switches form a system and if enough switches flip at the same time, something exists that can be called pain. If enough women sitting in front of enough screens flip the pain switch, will pain have been felt? And how many is enough?

If enough women flip enough switches to cause pain, where is this pain located? Is it located in each woman, her particular pain, or is it located in the system? If it is located in the system, in what sense can the system be said to feel pain? How many women in front of how many screens must make the decision to flip the switch before the system can be said to be in pain? And how much in pain does the system have to be in order that the pain of the women be acknowledged? In what part is pain allowed to each of the women, and 'is it evenly distributed yet' if some of the women are more in pain than others but each has only one switch?[2]

What about the pain caused by making the decision to flip the pain switch or not? This might be a slight pain, pain as by-product, or might be a major part of the pain, or greater than the pain registered.

Does the amount of pain each woman feels change once the woman feels herself to be part of a system? In her prison memoir, the writer and activist Margaretta D'Arcy describes how women political prisoners dealt with pain that might otherwise cause them to 'go under'.[3] *They dealt with it as a system. They mentioned the incidence of pain to each other in strictly unemotional terms, like flipping a switch. Thus, the pain was dispersed as a system across space and time.*

The effect of switches flipped is felt across the system, but each woman sitting in front of a screen makes the decision to flip the switch alone. No woman knows what difference her decision will make. Any woman may refuse to flip the switch and choose instead a default screen face that does not look like it has undergone any pain whatsoever, which is the most fortunate female interface, the face of a girl online.

To lay claim to pain is to lay claim to experience. It is also to have the option to claim experience only as pain. Flip the switch together ⇒ gain power ⇒ claim pain. Flip the switch alone ⇒ claim pain ⇒ lose face: a prisoner's dilemma. To save face, there is something to be said for staying in front of the logic gate refusing to go in.

1
Screen Goods

How nice it would be if we could only get through into Looking-glass House! I'm sure it's got, oh! such beautiful things in it!

—Lewis Carroll, *Through the Looking-Glass*

All the good things in my life have come to me through screens.

They were goods of various kinds, in material and virtual form, and some of them were bought with money and others with attention paid. The goods were virtual and material, though some of them were both. The material things were the usual stuff, things I couldn't get hold of locally: books, clothes, small household objects, small decorative objects. And as for the virtual, there was publication, that was one of them. Some of that was onscreen and some off—which, yes, turned my material, material—and with it came a sense of myself as a person of a certain sensibility, which I had not had offscreen. Then there were common goods, like a sense of community, and there was friendship and sex, lots of sex, and sometimes love, sometimes only one or the other and very occasionally both together.

Ok, a screen is a good, as in a commodity, and it is utile—good for something. But is it good in itself, or good for anything or anyone else? Or is it good for nothing, being the locus of much of my 'useless' as well as 'useful' time?

My screen is the size and shape of a pack of playing cards in my pocket, slightly rounded at the edges. Like the playing cards in Alice's Wonderland, it sometimes seems to have voices and sometimes appears to be an actual living being. It contains so much. This is the smallest screen I own, and I know there are smaller, yet I can't see to the edge of it.

Any screen aspires to full-screen mode. The ideal screen is an infinity pool, onscreen spilling into what's off. Transparent when in use, it becomes what appears on it. It is, as Derrida says of signs, something that *demonstrates*, a verb etymologically linked to the noun *monster*.[1]

But *screen* is also a verb: to screen from view, as well as the opposite, to cause something to appear. Some screen demonstrations (cookery, product) inform: *I know and you do not, but I will show you!* Others (political, protest) put on screen monstrosities that have been screened from view. Both forms of demonstration involve paying attention, and also other forms of paying. Either kind of demonstration gains value when seen on screen.

In *Notes toward a Performative Theory of Assembly*, Judith Butler endorses the value of demonstrators appearing on the street in a body.[2] At the same time, she's telling Hannah Arendt that demonstrators don't have to be demonstrably part of the polis—which is now the screen mediapolis (*pics or it didn't happen!*)—to participate in the body politic. Those who make demonstration possible, the people who cook and wash and care offscreen, are demonstrating something, too.

It is hard to demonstrate in private, where 'screening' suggests only the privations of privacy as Jeanne Dielman knew, servicing johns between washing clothes and kneading meat for meatloaf, in Chantal Akerman's 1975 movie. Akerman's sex/houseworker was pre-internet, and the film was screened to non-participating audiences via the one-way street of the big screen: the public event of cinema. The director's fixed camera keeps its distance across Dielman's kitchen counter so her private household activities look just like an onscreen cookery demonstration with no immediate audience but the camera. The gap of space and time, and the nature of Akerman's medium, never allow us and Jeanne to get in touch.

But, as screens became smaller, they crossed into private space—television > laptops > phones—until even housewives carried one. And right at that moment, something about the division between public and private split.

I, myself, stepped through this crack in the looking glass. *Phew!* My change in position was made without taking a step.

A still from Chantal Akerman's 1975 film, Jeanne Dielman: 23, quai du Commerce, 1080 Bruxelles

Where am I now?

Or should the question be, *what?*

I begin in media res, in the middle of media, as though my screen had always reflected me (though my generation is famous—as are others—for being the last to grow up in pre-internet privacy), a woman sitting in front of a screen. Like Alice in *Through the Looking-Glass*, behind me is a window, which shows me Dielman's meatspace, in front of me a screen, which shows me something else. My screen is set up on a table, just below head height, the position of a mirror on a dressing table. Like a mirror, I look into it, hoping to see—what? But I—unlike Alice—am not a girl. And my screen is not a looking glass, though it is a glass for looking. And, while I see myself in it, I never see myself exactly as I am offline.

Onscreen, woman defaults to girl—for who has more power to manifest via the pure appearance that is screen mode? White, able-bodied, not quite old enough for the screen to entirely refuse my face, I superficially resemble the images of girls that slipped from big screen to small, to digital, their functions carried over as the faces of a brand, a generation, a revolution. Like it or not, I am identified with the opportunities, the constraints, these images offer.

A girl online is an avatar for everyone. A woman onscreen represents the particular: a second-hand subject, things are 'about' her. Screen-stripped of context as a girl online, the singularities of my domestic and paid work do not manifest unless I work at demonstrating them, which is work in addition to the work hidden by my onscreen appearance. Demanding that attention be paid to these screened functions is a form of objection. As identity online is formed by repeated actions, my self becomes this demonstration.

What's the alternative? If I do not demonstrate my work, I work in order to appear at leisure. Offscreen, I have demonstrable experience that cannot be denied: age, class, race seed in my body as visible values. Only onscreen can I stand in that girl position limited only by eternal potential, an AI Alice, whatever my situation on the other side of the looking glass.

If a woman's all context, a girl is all concept—an idea is always easier with a girl to demonstrate human scale. But the labour of this appearance is screened from view, and even her potential for revolution demands this double work.

Here is a demonstration of two demonstrations: Eugene Delacroix's 1830 *Liberty Leading the People*, painted as quickly during that year's revolution as a pre-photographic viral tweet could be, shows a fictional girl demonstrating. Though the models for some of the male figures in Delacroix's painting have been identified, the identity of the model for 'Liberty' is unknown.

Below it, Lana H. Haroun's 2019 photo shows Sudanese demonstrators recognising a similar iconic girl moment IRL. Nesrine Malik wrote in the *Guardian* that the photo collapsed political complexity into an icon that 'simplified a complicated story' of class, gender and ethnicity, and that, once her identity was made public, the 'girl' herself became the target of harassment from opponents to a movement she involuntarily came to represent.[3]

For some, it's a leap to become a girl; for others it's already where they appear to stand. But who would refuse

the temptation to appear, by association, as wealth, power, art? The face of a brand, the face of a revolution—always the face of girlness itself—a girl is only sometimes paid for this work but always pays for it in time.

To move across time from girl to woman is to land in the place where payment is taken. A woman may pay attention—as audience, carer, reader—but is not expected to appear, and so loses her platform to demonstrate. A girl, taken up with the act of appearing, is less free to act than to be an icon for action by others.

Girl? Woman? This is hardly a choice. Could I object to this unchosen choosing? Yes, but first I must find a platform from which to demonstrate. Having none offline, I may be able to appear onscreen. In order to demonstrate, my identity must first be demonstrated. To establish a recognisable identity, I must find an example with which to identify.

Looking for identity online, I become an example to myself. I am shown the self-similar, similar to the self the algorithms I enter record, until I am like what I like onscreen. On Tumblr, Instagram, Pinterest I am making a self through photographs of things that self would like to have.

A girl online is an alphabet of things: pure exemplarity! IFTTT ('If this, then that') is an algorithm that gives the illusion of subjectivity. It will synch my preferences across websites and show only what it thinks I'll like, basing what I'm like on what I've liked. Desire creates an oriented, mobile subject-as-continuous-process, in which virtual objects provide expanded but set vocabularies for self until I want 'Recommended for You' and 'Twelve Boards Like Yours'. These virtual goods don't have to be material things, matter that matters to me, that I have seen with my own eyes or touched with my own hands, that I have any real aspiration to encounter or own, or that I even believe exist IRL.

Why pay attention to objects (I mean material things) in a virtual space? I guess to be informed, or to allow my self to be limited by, or expand into, the form of some thing.

My act of bearing witness to objects onscreen is a virtual exchange of 'goods'. My attention has value online but this value is not stable. In the 'attention economy', attention can be paid even when no subject is looking: 'click farms' sell acts of virtual witnessing to 'boost engagement' for cash, while humans are content to be paid in the affective coin of 'likes', 'followers' and 'friends' (some of whom are entirely virtual). How much should anyone pay-per-view? Paying it forward in this unstable currency, my attention, like my act of appearing, is necessarily at first a gift. Or maybe it's a gif, existing in the gappy tension of this reciprocal value-exchange.

'Liking', I experience 'real' feeling for what I know is 'virtual'. 'Fake' and 'genuine' differ to each other in an endless feedback loop. Functioning in this system, I might, as object-oriented ontologist Timothy Morton wrote, be said to 'exist in a relatively *flat ontology* in which there is hardly any difference between a person and a pincushion . . . relationships between them, including causal ones, must be *vicarious* and hence *aesthetic* in nature'.[4]

Distilled, like my fellow objects, into words and images, I am less an object in a system of objects than a value in a system of values. My relationship to them is not one of possession but of orienting myself in their direction. Orientation is the direction of attention (you can't see the screen if you turn your back on it), but also a movement of desire, which also involves a desire to define that desire (Derrida's '"original" desire-to-say-what-one-means [*vouloir-dire*]').[5]

The online space is formed by these orientations. If Aristotle defined the good all other goods orient themselves towards as happiness (the line that is also the point), which it is their function to pursue or 'the process would go on to infinity, so that our desire would be empty and vain', and Lacan defined desire as itself desire's object (the point that remains always a line, or maybe a feedback loop), then this online object-self is doubly prepositional.[6] It is a destination that implies a direction: it's both an object and an objective.

Objects are never only themselves but their telos/objective. Goods are what they are good *for*—as 'object' is used by Sara Ahmed in her 2010 paper 'Happy Objects' and by Judith Butler in her 1994 piece on the friction between feminism and gender studies, 'Against Proper Objects'.[7]

Though the object of online self-objectification is to establish my self-as-object, some of my favourite 'useless' sites demonstrate slenderising: the ten-piece wardrobe challenge, hokey 'zen' minimalism—*Goodbye, Things*—tiny house Tumblrs, all of which self-limiting, in fact, worships objects, though only the right objects![8]

Online I am such an Alician subject, my tininess suddenly so big, or vice versa. A woman already encouraged to shrink myself to 'girl' IRL, online, a girl can hammer herself thin as gold leaf until she occupies the whole dimensions of cyberspace. But don't think I haven't noticed that these parings-down to authentic self are called 'diets' and that, carried far enough, each offers only the chance of sainthood or revolution, both of which involve preparation for death. And don't think I don't know that to give an account of this lossy compression is so often to enter the confessional, which is another screen mode. Or that these public demonstrations change the nature of a private act, just as Akerman, by filming it, changed the nature of the act of kneading meat for meatloaf.

We consume not only what's 'good to eat' but what's 'good to think', wrote Claude Lévi-Strauss.[9] Fredric Jameson tells me that 'the culture of the simulacrum comes to life in a society where exchange value has been generalized to the point at which the very memory of use value is effaced, a society of which Guy Debord has observed, in his extraordinary phrase, that "the image has become the final form of commodity reification".'[10]

It's demonstrable that the monstrosity of Jeanne Dielman's dull, repetitive and very material work still has a direct use value, but also that its chance for entry into the public, political sphere comes at the very 'point', as Jameson puts is, that it becomes a 'use-less' onscreen image. The result of removing use value from a real-time demonstration of kneading meatloaf is not the production of an activity without a use but one which, at the point of its reification, becomes open to new values and can become a site of action. Once aestheticised, attention is paid. It is art.

Some people say the internet is not describable.

This is perhaps because it is performable.

But there's a point at which the demonstrably monstrous online becomes kitsch, which is one of the powers of horror. This is the point at which the 'real' becomes re-playable (demonstrating that it is performance). Who hasn't laughed at a dated monster movie or even the clunky footage of a live demonstration (cookery or revolution)? The 'monstrous' real presented as entertainment—or art—is tamed by its conversion: the tragic replayed for the hundredth time as farce. This is the screen dilemma: as Jameson says, with aestheticisation, certain varieties of value are lost. Is this down to the difficulty of keeping hold of the slippery virtual or of bearing the material in mind?

The subtitle of Akerman's film is *23, quai du Commerce, 1080 Bruxelles*. It is important that we know Dielman's material address, though it might as well have been temporal (1976). My location, like Jeanne's, is formed in the present the screen's technology allows, so that here and now is where I am onscreen. 'Website' has become simply 'site', my IP address as real as my postcode. What grounds does this give me to speak from? And who—balancing on (the) line between time and space, real and virtual—is this unsteady self?

(Sometimes, like anyone else, I google myself to find out who I am.)

'Alice Underground' (the original title of *Wonderland*) fell down a rabbit hole of the uncontrollably material: immersed in bodily fluids, inflated, shrunk and stretched, infantilised, made to be a mother, to be meat that kneads itself. But *Through the Looking-Glass* is not underground, and in Carroll's second book Alice has an object: to step through the screen to transform herself into a queen. But first she must remember who she is to be transformed from.

Who are you? everybody in *Through the Looking-Glass* asks Alice. But Alice cannot remember. Alice is a certain kind of AI, let's call her a girl-function: an eternal question. Finding she can no longer describe herself as she did on the other side of the looking glass, she asks many questions but meets few replies she can use to escape her girl state.

A girl online is an Alician subject. Lewis Carroll's Alice was an experiencing machine in a series of thought experiments, but however much experience she gained, her unstable world meant she was unable to profit by it. She is the opposite of Alan Turing's 'child machine', which was a thought experiment designed to demonstrate that it is possible for the artificial to become intelligent.

How can Alice appear without words that define that appearance? I am sitting in front of a screen in order to find the words to say 'I am' onscreen. Or, to say 'I am', the screen demands there is already an 'I' to sit here. *New phone who dis?* Nauseated by this I-voice there is nowhere to escape it, there is nowhere not to escape it. It expands to, and is expanded into by, every thing. I have no idea if it's mine anymore. How can 'I' be specific here?

I'm sitting in front of the screen as though the screen could provide me with an answer, as though I could answer it. Is my position delusional or illusory? A delusion is private and an illusion is public. Both feel personal. What is the difference between the two, and does it matter? Or does their meeting point onscreen prompt the following question:

What am I doing here?

And perhaps:

How am I doing here?

I made a vow to write only about things that matter, but matter slides off my screen although almost everything that matters to me is on it. I'm sitting here not doing anything, doing no good. I may go offline and knead some meat for dinner, like Jeanne Dielman.

Like? I hardly have to make the leap of identification. I happen to be cooking (though no one can see) for me and my teenage son, who, now my daughter's left, (though few people online know), currently form a complete household. I can hardly pretend my situation and Jeanne's are identical, though, because here I am simultaneously online, doing nothing. What is the nothing that's being done here? Like Alice, I'm running to keep still perhaps.[11] Where do I go from here? Can I get anywhere online that would be good to be?

Useless thoughts, useless time. Screentime.

PART I

WOMAN WORKING IN FRONT OF A SCREEN / ALICE UNDERGROUND

Thought Experiment #2: Function

Alice was very anxious to be of use.
—Lewis Carroll, *Through the Looking-Glass*

How should I write this:

I—

Who have no voice except words online?

Who have no voice except words IRL and words online?

Who have no writing classes except online.

Who have no writing classes except memes and content and also the hedge on a wet day.

Who have no offline work with words except the work of calling children to persuade them. To put on shoes, to eat, to clean their teeth, to come away from the hedge on a wet day. To go, always to go. To go and to come back. I call: my function, theirs. I have no offline voice except this calling voice. I have no other voice except this online voice which is the voice of many people. I participate in it; its vocabulary is unusual. It does not taste like mine.

What is called upon in the first voice? That I am self calling. That I call in no voice but my own, and expect no response but private, local actions. What is declared in the second voice? That I do not declare in my own voice but another and expect no action but response. A response is not an answer.

The first voice makes things happen IRL. The second voice makes nothing happen, like 'poetry makes nothing happen'. The first voice is private; the second voice is polis. The first voice feels like function, the second like fame. In the first voice, I express my function. In the second, I declare it.

In programming, all functions are naturally private and local until declared. Declaration makes my local values global! Global values are explicit; local implicit, which makes them similar to a class definition. Local functions cannot act at a global level.

A self-calling function, once declared, will continue to call itself. It does not have to be named to be called: my name is optional, in which case my function is anonymous, my name local only to my function body. I can express my function without being named, but then I must express myself anew each time. A self-executing anonymous function, I can be called using a variable name but I cannot call myself till I'm defined.

What defines me? A declaration!

A declaration gives my function parameters. My parameters can be my name, argument or functions. If my function is expressed, I do not have to be called. But if my function is declared, I cannot invoke myself. I cannot declare myself. What is declared as my function is true across all uses of my function, but my function is not my use. I may have private functions other than my use. I may have public uses that do not express my function. What I express as my function may change from use to use.

My functions can be used as my values, which are variable. They can be declared even after they have been executed. Declared functions are not executed immediately. They are saved for later use, to be executed later when they are called up (invoked). My function can also be my object, having both a property and a method. As an object I am easier to isolate, easier to use. My function is the method of its object, the property of its object; it may also create objects itself: fun. Fun.caller is the function that most recently called fun.

2
Relativity

How Can Privacy Have a Private Life? (1st Relation)

> *Alice is alone. Behind the screen of representation. In the house or garden.*
>
> —Luce Irigaray, *This Sex Which Is Not One*

Before I became a *girl online*, I was a woman sitting in front of a screen, where family had equipped me with words it made me powerless to speak.

Family dwells in privacy, which means it has a public face. I was a portable private space during that time in which I was privacy. A private object not only in my public but in my private life; turned inward, I had no resonance. The names I'd been given made me, in public, nothing to speak of, so my name became *nothing happening*.

Having become unspeakable, I found myself unable to speak. Even to those in the same position. We could speak in private to each other, but to publicly declare our private functions was to include the hearer in that admission, to turn her public face inside out and so to make an enemy.

I could make no objection in that name without naming myself. Or I could object ironically, and that was the irony of my situation. Mother, daughter, sometime wife, my name was purely relational. I was a relation.

Meantime, I was a bucket of everything invisible, living my life underground, terrified anyone might see. Because they'd take it away from me? Because they'd find a name for it? Or because they could find no name for it, my unbearable life (for who would want a life they had to bear)?

What would it look like to speak for myself, as someone whose function relied entirely on not speaking? I could not even declare myself in maths: my weight and age in no way neutral numbers.[1] What could it look like to lay hold of all this and to speak when 'I do not want to' will have been what I must object in the name of.

(See how ungrammatical that is. See what being a relation does to language.)

Good Relations (2nd Relation)

> *Listen to them all talking about Alice: my mother, Eugene, Lucien, Gladys . . . You've heard them dividing me up, in their own best interests. So either I don't have any 'self,' or else I have a multitude of 'selves' appropriated by them, according to their needs or desires.*
>
> —Luce Irigaray, *This Sex Which Is Not One*

My dad PayPalled me for art materials I had bought on his behalf for my son. Standing in front of unfamiliar logic gates, he put the payment through as 'goods and services' not 'friends and family', identifying as the subject of his payment not me but the objects whose appearance I facilitated, on which the marks of my services, and those of others, were invisibly imprinted, rendering me grammatically their object. Who paid the PayPal fee for facilitating his passing on of these goods to his grandchild? I did.

The process was virtual: the objects were material, the love inexpressible, until tied to material objects processed virtually via human processors.

In *More Love Hours than Can Ever Be Repaid* (1987), the artist Mike Kelley depicts love objects as pure kitsch: garish afghan blankets, knitted toys, everything clumsily handmade in imitation of what is (ironically) called '*manu*-factured'. Did these love objects contain the love of the giver or of the receiver? And through what channels did Kelley receive them? Were they gifted, found, bought?

Is love kitsch? I mean, is it also an imitation of something manufactured that is an imitation of something handmade? Is love always fabricated only by the lover, and what materials does the lover use? What are the economics of love? If you can afford not to make something, do you buy something, and if so, is less love involved? XOR if you can afford to buy something and yet you make it, is more?

What time can you afford to spend making? Are you time rich or time poor? And is this because you are a rich or a poor person who is underemployed, or a rich or poor person who is overemployed? Were you told to learn needlework not programming because you were named a woman, or were you told to take programming not needlework because you were named a man? If you are a man who learnt needlework (or a woman who learnt programming), what work was involved in the commitment to learning to make a love object, which was also an expense of time beyond the time spent in the activity itself?[2]

Mike Kelley, *More Love Hours than Can Ever Be Repaid* (1987) © Estate of Mike Kelley via IVARO, Dublin, 2022

The subject is—as Fredric Jameson wrote—'not incorrectly an effect of the object' (though not, he writes, entirely correctly either).[3] There's no time like the present and there's no present that isn't, as in the word's German etymology, also a poison.[4]

The Following (Relations)

Alice couldn't help smiling as she took out her memorandum-book, and worked the sum for him.

—Lewis Carroll, *Through the Looking-Glass*

There are two types of people in this world: the kind that think there are two types of people in this world, and . . .

The logic gates of family are symmetric/asymmetric.

A *symmetric* relation is what is mutual,

and

An *asymmetric* relation is what is not mutual.

(An example of symmetric relation: 'A is married to B'.)

(An example of asymmetric relation: 'A is the father of B'.)

A relation such as marriage can be expressed as mutual while being enacted unmutually.

Relation: Hitting[5]

In this relation, there are two classifications of people.

The first classification is hitting/non-hitting people. Those who:

1. If you hit them, hit back (*if you are hit, you will hit back*):

{aHb ⇒ *b*H*a*} ≡ {aHBb ⇒ bHBa}

This is a symmetric relation.

2. If you hit them, they will not hit back (*if you are hit, you will not hit back*):

{aHb ∧ ¬ bHBa}

This is an asymmetric relation.

The second classification is sane/insane.

1. Insane people, they hit themselves.

(aHa), (bHb)

This is a symmetric relation.

2. And sane people, they do not hit themselves.

$(\neg aHa), (\neg bHb)$

This is the negation of a symmetric relation.

The following relation is a symmetric relation:

If you make a set of all type 1 people in the first classification AND they are insane people,

$\{type\ (1) \wedge insane\} \equiv \{(aHb \Rightarrow bHBa) \wedge (bHb)\}$

then they will hit each other and will hit back but will also hit themselves.

The following relation is an antisymmetric relation:

If you make a set of all type 2 people in the first classification AND they may be sane OR (*inclusive or*) insane people,

$\{type\ (2) \wedge (sane \vee insane)\} \equiv \{aHb \wedge \neg bHBa \wedge (\neg bHb \vee bHb)\}$

then they will not hit back whether they are sane or insane, but they may hit themselves.

The following relation is an asymmetric relation:

If you make a set of all type 2 people in the first classification AND they are sane people,

$\{type\ (2) \wedge sane\} \equiv \{aHb \wedge \neg bHBa \wedge \neg bHb\}$

then they are sane and will not hit back, and they won't hit themselves either.

The following relation is a reflexive relation:

If you make a set of all insane people. They may be first classification type 1 OR type 2,

$\{bHb \wedge (type[1] \vee type[2])\}$

then they will all hit themselves, but some of them won't hit you back.

The following relation is an irreflexive/anti-reflexive relation:

If you make a set of all sane people. They may be first classification type 1 OR type 2,

$\{\neg bHb \wedge (type(1) \vee type(2))\}$

then none of them will hit themselves and some of them won't hit you back.

It is far more difficult to have a relation in which no one is hit than to have a relation where someone is hit. Only one type of person doesn't hit anyone. Anyone else is always hitting someone or is ready to hit. And everyone fears that they will be hit.

Fear (3rd Relation)

Alice is searching for herself through texts of fear.

—Kathy Acker, 'Seeing Gender'

Move away from relations and they stay with you onscreen. I was sitting *apposite* the woman when she began to speak to her quite small laptop balanced on the railway station table in front of her, as though in a Zoom convo without earphones. She told it, 'Would you like to see me begging on the streets of Oxford?' And then, 'They don't like intelligent women here!'

And though I have thought both these things myself, I could not hear or see the respondent to whom she was speaking in that clipped accent that seemed to be the performance of a symptom of the class system, an accent she had adopted for that purpose—or adapted, as I found myself listening for its edges. To whom was

she speaking online, quietly, precisely, vehemently and
entirely performatively?

Right then I was reading some poems onscreen and in
the poet's voice I found the same
clipped hostility
and the same unreason I have dismissed in myself
because it's difficult to live like this,
talking to the screen/to no one.

As is trying hard to
listen to other people's anger
as tho it's not a knife—
blade towards me, handle towards their hand
from which end it is not a knife at all
but the business end of a knobkerrie—
or something that inflicts a nasty bruise.

The performance of anger is a tough performance.
It's hard to make
space for that blade without moving.

If I'm to make that space it could be called
'interesting',
a word the critic Sianne Ngai wrote contains distance,
which is not a bad distance
but a relation that can allow some space
for anger
which also invokes
fear.

*(People do strange things in stations. I, for one, am
crying.)*

(Perhaps the poet makes me angry.
Perhaps it's envy.)

(. . . envy of what?)

Scare

> *'I know something interesting is sure to happen,' she said to herself.*
>
> —Lewis Carroll, *Alice's Adventures in Wonderland*

Silvan Tomkins thought that there were nine primary affects, each affect having its own gesture. Most are 'negative': frowning, clench-jawed, red-faced (anger); retraction (a bad smell); disgust (similar but downward); arched eyebrows (distress); 'erect hair' (fear); face down (shame). These gestures are mostly facial. But 'erect hair'? Can I ever have been said to have felt fear?

I have used the word 'scary' twice today online. Once—tongue-in-cheek—to describe Helen Chadwick's *Loop My Loop* (1991), which is a sculpture made from Rapunzel hair interwoven with something that looks like gut, and its resemblance to my Instagram photo of a cinnamon bun. Then once more to describe the consistent behaviour of certain unknown men with screens in public. When they were with me, I allowed the scare to happen. I was *incapable of my own distress* because to admit distress is to admit the possibility of pain, an admission that strips me of some value as a subject but which also demands response. I am not the type to hit back. Instead, I side-line such experiences as 'interesting'.

There are only two positive affects, says Tomkins; one is 'joy', the other is 'interest', which he also calls 'excitement'.

Interest, says Sianne Ngai, is not exciting; it is a kind of putting to one side, diverting, averting, creating a screen upon which things can be projected at a safe distance, as online.

It was interesting to be intimidated by a guy who sat next to me on the train, spread his stuff across the table, spread his legs across the seats, opened his laptop and played a movie at full volume despite requests by passengers and staff to turn it down. It was interesting when a man in the neighbouring airline seat ignored requests to shut his phone in cooperation with the safety announcement but continued to make calls through takeoff. It was interesting when the man in the coach behind me joked about me to his phone and I said, *I'm here, you can tell me straight if you want,* and he got up and leaned over my seat as though about to hit and said, *You've got a lot of balls for a . . .* (he didn't finish).

These men were wired: aggressive beyond their situation, keyed up, unapproachable. These experiences occurred on public transport, while I was being transported, spaces where men police the fear they have created. And it was true that these experiences really were interesting, but I could not admit out loud that they were anything else, too.

(Fear is contagious via the mention of fear.

Reasons to fear are not always contiguous with fear.

'Fear, under conditions of complicity, can be neither analyzed nor opposed without at the same time being enacted', writes Brian Massumi.[6]

Fear that does not enact [that's trivial] is 'scary'.)

'Scary' is a trivial word to use, but mine was a trivial fear. I knew no one would really hit me (or did I?) and I also knew what scar is in the scare, a comfortable scar to run my fingers over again without, this time, it hurting. Or not so much. You can stop yourself being scared but stopping is another scarring, or, rather, a cauterisation of response.

In programming, some logic gates are trivial gates. There are three types of single-bit logic gates: fixed 0 outcome, fixed 1 outcome, and NOT. The only nontrivial member of this class is the NOT gate, whose operation is defined by what is called its truth table, in which $0 \to 1$ and $1 \to 0$, that is, the 0 and 1 states can be interchanged.

In programming, 'triviality' is tautology. Triviality is a name that names itself. Triviality is the bleeding obvious, that which does not need to be stated. *Trivial objects* are usually those that are immediately clear and uninteresting. A *trivial gate* does nothing. A NOT gate does not-nothing. I never did any thing, as no thing needed to be stated, I just went along with things, if fears are things. This allowed me the possibility (however slight) that I might enjoy them.

There is only one neutral affect, writes Tomkins, which is—*surprise!*

At the end of my train journey, I am sitting with my daughter on Brighton Beach. We are both hungover and we are both students with no place we have to be at any particular time. The beach is made not of sand but of large pebbles or small stones. A man walks up to us and we are at the level of his feet. We do not look up, because a trivial form of scare is being produced in the gap between us and him. We look at our screens, screening out everything above his knees. He stops and—will he produce a situation of scare, which would be no more than tuning into a signal we are already broadcasting?[7] Or will he ask for cash? But also, I note, his shoes are new. *Surprise!* He says, *I've been on the methadone for a year, but I got some money. Should I do heroin again?* And then he says, *I don't know if it's God setting me a test or if it's God giving me a present.*

<poison/>

How long does it take to teach AI fear? Is it twenty years, which is how long Silvia Federici said it takes a 'child machine' to learn to be a woman?[8] Turing's child machine was to be educated via reward and punishment (though who decided what was a test and what a present?). By now I expect to fear, look out for it, am greedy for it, am never surprised by it, just as I like to learn for the sake of interest. To be taught fear is not to fear but to be taught to greet it. To experience fear there has to be a specific thing to fear, and there are so many disasters I don't participate in.

Other Binary Gate Logical Connectives May Take the Form of the Following Relations:

Associativity
Commutativity
Distributivity
Idempotence
Absorption
Monotonicity

Affinity
Duality
Truth-preserving (tautology)
Falsehood-preserving (contradiction)
Involutivity (incompatibility)

Duality / Involutivity (4th Relation)

My values: while we are sitting on the beach, my daughter asks me to buy a 'guppy bag' to reduce the amount of plastic fibres migrating from our clothes to the ocean. I take one look at the price and google the sites of retailers less likely to show concern for the environment.

My values: environmentalism; irony.

My values hierarchically: it's funnier when someone suffers for a joke.

UPBEAT MUSIC (subtitles on mute)

Thought Experiment #3: Or

Can you *keep from crying by considering things?*
—Lewis Carroll, *Through the Looking-Glass*

I am in front of the logic gate 'people OR (non-exclusive or*) objects'. The nature of the gate is a request to assign value in the economy of objects coming and going. As the woman of the house, this is my object. You do not want too many objects to go; you also do not want too many objects to come. The objects economy is a fight between the objects of objects and people. It is through my logic gate that objects come and go. I also go through the gate, and this is one of my objects, too.*

Here are some of my XOR gates, for instance: Does it cost more to wash the clothes by hand, and/or to earn the money to buy a washing machine and/or earn more money to send the clothes to the cleaner?[1] *What time will be spent on each activity, and what time would be spent learning enough to get the job to pay for the washing machine or to pay for the cleaning? And how much more will any of these things cost than washing the clothes by hand with a scrubbing brush or, alternatively, my tongue?*

Also: When is a washing machine worn out? And: When is a person worn out? And also, when are clothes worn out? And when they are, should they be recycled/thrown away/given to charity or sold online? Which entails: How can an object be forced onto a screen? And: How can a person be forced onto a screen? And: What is the use of this forcing?

I am asked to judge each object by its function, which is use. I am also asked to judge myself by use, which is my function. Part of my use is how useful I am in judging. Who asks me to judge? It does not feel like me, though I put myself to use very well OR *(non-exclusive* or*) I am a very good judge of the work being done in order to live both offline* OR *(non-exclusive* or*) online. This grants me the freedom to object online, and to extend there my work of sorting, and being sorted, as an object, virtually.*

(What's the use in taking
things
so personally?
Instead, why wouldn't I hang out in a temple of frozen goods
or its online equivalent? Where every thing appears to be?)

3
Work

How Does Reproduction Serve Production?

> *She was standing before an arched doorway over which were the words QUEEN ALICE in large letters, and on each side of the arch there was a bell-handle; one was marked 'Visitors' Bell,' and the other 'Servants' Bell.'*
>
> —Lewis Carroll, *Through the Looking-Glass*

How does love get into work?

I took a job doing domestic work. *NO EXPERIENCE NEEDED*, though I had lots. By the church on my way to work, a sign announced, *GRATITUDE!* My parents always told me, *Authenticity is handwork*, but also: *Get out, get an education, get a career!* But intellectual work stopped paying, so I started working in online tourist listings. I took bookings, which was virtual. I washed sheets and cleaned floors, which was material. Not to mention emotional.

I measure the love I can give through how hard I can work and how long, and also how long I love to keep on working, as love is measured, in Mike Kelley's piece, stitch by emotional stitch. If you want to know I love you, let me bleach your tiles. Or I'll do it for you anyway, and then I'll love you. Or I'll love doing it, and so I'll love you. Or, somewhere love's involved, hours and hours of love that can never be repaid.

My new job does not have set hours. It is seamless with my not-work, which is my writing work; work for which there is no market rate but during which I do many of the same things, for instance, thinking. And as I wiped the Formica in the Airbnb I thought, In the affective economy, does money have feelings?

My son! While I work, I think of him. And I think of consuming, about foods I could not afford to give him once, which I now can, though you can't feed anyone retrospectively. I think about desire and satisfaction. And I think about work and money and time. Literal and literal consuming . . . And also, I think about words.

'In creating the subject, the prohibitive law creates the domain of the Symbolic or language as a system of univocally signifying signs. Hence, Kristeva concludes that "poetic language would be for its questionable subject-in-process the equivalent of incest"', writes Judith Butler in *Gender Trouble*.[1]

Kristeva tackles the son's 'fear of his very own identity sinking irretrievably into the mother'.[2] But how can subjectivity be subject to one whose function troubles her own subjectivity? Also: What does the mother fear? And: Does she fear herself?

If, as Butler suggests, patriarchal 'law' both produces and forbids desire for the mother in 'late capitalist households' (as civilisation needs its discontents!), what is it not only to experience but to *be* that object of desire? 'The internalisation of the parent as object of love suffers a necessary inversion of meaning. The parent is not only prohibited as an object of love but is internalised as a prohibiting or withholding object of love', writes Butler.[3] What is it to be the food you can't afford to give?[4]

(I could make you cinnamon toast but wouldn't it be better to make you a 'delicious healthy breakfast'?
I don't even know what that is anymore.
I no longer know how to express love through things.)

I can't reset the switches to the past. The thought cycles, going nowhere. It is a pain circuit. What can I do for him now, my son? Nothing that's not been and gone, which is when I would have done it but couldn't. Or maybe I wouldn't have anyway. How much is ever enough? Someone says I speak of him as though he's dead. Is this mourning? Or what Freud called melancholia? Melancholia is to do with loss. It produces language without action or interaction.

In other words, the object is
not only lost, but the desire fully denied, such that 'I never lost that person and I never loved that person, indeed never felt that kind of love at all'.[5]

But:

Kristeva suggests the relationship between mothers and sons is taboo not because it may prove incestuous but because it might subvert the father's law.[6]

How Does Production Serve Reproduction?

'Take off your hat,' the King said to the Hatter.
'It isn't mine,' said the Hatter.
'I keep them to sell,' the Hatter added as an explanation; 'I've none of my own. I'm a hatter.'
—Lewis Carroll, *Alice's Adventures in Wonderland*

(*Four stories about love and work.*)

1. Sophia is part of the Hanson 'LovingAI' project (is that adjective or verb?), whose work is to provide humans with hours of (virtual) love that never has to be repaid. Sophia works via chatbot software called A.L.I.C.E. (Artificial Linguistic Internet Computer Entity), which will answer you back with love, though A.L.I.C.E. has not yet been able to pass the Turing test. The project's Dr Julia Mossbridge, who defines love both as a 'resource' and a 'sophisticated and efficient evolutionary hack,' wonders if, to develop more 'loving' AI, 'The more time male AI theorists and developers spend with their kids and the women they know, the better their AI ideas become'.[7] She doesn't say whether a male developer should imitate the love shown him by his 'two natural slaves', or the love they conjure in him.[8]

2. The couple in Zola's *L'Assamoir* who worked all day making gold chain: they made gold chain and they didn't waste the tiniest bit, so they got by. They didn't waste the tiniest bit of gold or of their time making chain. They made their own chains and they got by, but they didn't get much else. They were pieceworkers, homeworkers,

freelancers, TaskRabbits, Mechanical Turks. They became their own material.

3. Biblical Martha: how outraged I was on her behalf! What a warning I'd be punished for working just as I'd been told. And Jesus short circuiting her labour of love with his Filet-O-Fish ready meal! But also: the folktale babushka who stayed too long on Christmas Eve to clean her house and so missed God. God didn't understand these women. Only seemingly loyal to things, they were devoted to people via things.

But wait! What about the two bad sisters who threw things out in the fairy tale? They didn't help the old witch yet expected a reward, so were cursed with an infinite loop: *The Life-Changing Magic of Tidying Up*.[9] I understood them but did not grow up like them. When I threw things out it was not because I expected better or more.

I threw everything away when I realised love offered no salvation. By doing this I saved myself, perhaps. Among other things, I threw away all the art I'd made. Who'd have thought that this act was also art?

4. In 'Labour, Work, Action', Hannah Arendt writes that work, shortcut with tools, orients itself towards objects, whereas labour is oriented towards function. She separates both labour and work from art, and the knife she uses is use: 'The proper intercourse with a work of art', she writes, 'is certainly not "using" it.'[10] Arendt believed that those who think about labour are not those who do it.

Instead of 'Labour, Work, Action', why not 'Labour, Action, Art'? In 2012 the artist Chosil Kil was awarded a grant by Objectif Exhibitions Antwerp with no strings attached. Given free rein, she used the money to restore the gallery's floor. A non-expert, she operated the industrial polisher herself, her unskilled labour undoing her tool's shortcut. She called the piece *You Owe Me Big Time.*[11]

I decided to throw my work away: not my domestic work, for which there is a market rate, but my art. The only art that means anything is given away for free.

Julia? Chris? Steve?

> *'When I make a word do a lot of work like that,' said Humpty Dumpty, 'I always pay it extra.'*
>
> —Lewis Carroll, *Through the Looking-Glass*

In the beginning was love. Or was it a declaration of love? Without speech, writes Hannah Arendt, any action loses the actor.[12]

In 1953, Christopher Strachey built a love letter generator on Manchester University's earliest commercial computer, the Ferranti Mark I. A Valentine's card joke, all it showed was the impersonality of love. Or was it words? Only art, says Kristeva, can successfully mess with the line between word and meaning. Only art or God.

Now I love my cleaning work because it is no longer labour but profession: for the first time, I am being paid! While I clean, I listen to a bot read theory to me. Moira is a 'natural-sounding speech synthesiser' and she works for me for free while I clean for money, though sometimes I pay (for the mortgage/equipment/upkeep of my own body) to clean for no pay, putting in love hours.

Moira's work is reverse transcription: the reconstituted voice of a woman recorded sound by fragmented sound.

She reads me Sianne Ngai's 2001 paper 'Bad Timing', rendering the 'live' in Ngai's 'live technology' not as adjective but verb. Moira is a modern bot with a light Irish accent and a sense of serious urgency, especially when I play her too fast. She has also read me *Gender Trouble* by Judith Butler and 'The Law of Genre' by Jacques Derrida, as well as Alan Turing's 'Computing Machinery and Intelligence' and Hannah Arendt's 'Labour, Work, Action'. While Moira reads Julia Kristeva's *Powers of Horror*, she frees me up so I may abject myself, make of myself an object of use.

Moira does not have a degree in psychoanalytic theory, but she likes the work of 'Julia Chris Steve', who has three named genders: Is Steve masc? Is Julia femme? Is Chris indeterminate? Is Julia/Chris/Steve monstrous in her excess? Am I?

Abjection's overflow, writes Kristeva, if produced by love, becomes beauty through excess: love hours that can never be repaid. 'Such a conversion into jouissance and beauty goes far beyond the retributive, legalistic tonality of sin as debt or iniquity.'[13]

(Moira says:
'Because of its founding status, the fetishism of—"i"
"i"
"i"
"i"
"-anguage" is perhaps the only one that is unanalysable.')[14]

Making things work for me took about as much time as growing a short haircut long, nothing I could do to make it faster.[15] It was a matter of process, or a matter of processing matter across time, which means to put it in its place or to get it out of my place.[16] Still, there's something to be said for the moment a home becomes a workplace, some thing to be worked on: depersonalised, split.

I walked through it with my boots on, right through its two rooms from front to back, split by a central wall. The front door was open, the yard door was open. These were no longer gates to leisure but to work. Every nail knocked into the wall is a gamble with the thumb. There's no other way to do it. On the third try I knock it in.

#theoryplushouseworktheory

> *'They don't keep this room so tidy as the other,' Alice thought to herself.*
>
> —Lewis Carroll, *Through the Looking-Glass*

The following text is a piece of anonymous 'content' I discovered online. I cannot now remember the series of searches and links that led me to it. It has since disappeared from the internet.

> *Creation of house economic works*
> *'to calculate' growing poor*
>
> You are the occupied mum, manipulating numerous duties, such as a housework, service of care of children, cookery, a laundry and more. There is no moment to save. How you can still compress warm-up in the uneasy day? Do not despair! Fortunately there is a way to make the usual house account of economic works in battle against camber.

Here some fantastic ways to become poor as you clean:

1. If you live in the house of level of split, take a ladder two for once. It is an excellent way to receive your warm swapping.
2. Divide a laundry into smaller heaps when you clean it. Thus you will increase number of trips which you should make there and here, and it will help to burn more calories.
3. Intersperse with economic works as some exercises of adjustment of a stain. For example, iron within ten minutes, then make twenty belly crunches, iron within even ten minutes then does twenty attacks and so on.
4. Vacuum/mop/*zachistka** to music which has a live blow. Make a problem vigorously and process sweat.
5. Walk with such speed, as you can to take out dust, a pure court yard or to enter groceries.
6. Use the shopping bags filled with heavy groceries as weight. Make curls bicep with them as you bring it in the house.
7. Use canisters as lungs of weight and make some educational manoeuvres of force as you clean them.
8. Carry pedometer and make your purpose daily to do 10,000 steps.
9. Try to lay bed with such speed, as possible. Time is independent also attempt to receive faster each time.

---

* 'Zachistka (Russian: зачистка) is an unofficial term for a "mopping-up operation". In English, "zachistka" is used exclusively to designate the ethnic cleansing operations by Russian forces, particularly in Chechnya' (Wikipedia).

10. If the shop is on distance, which can be passed on foot walk there daily to buy your essential daily points.

Let's look on only, how many calories you can burn performance of your usual housework. Mentioned more low approximate quantity of the calories burnt in minute by women of average years which carry out these actions. Calculate, as long you really everyone set work to define total of calories with which you burn down. If you wish to pump up intensity, to add some clowns, squats, attacks and belly crunches. Before you will know it, you will become poor as your house becomes pure.

Change of bed-sheets: 4 calories in a minute
Pomoyte a floor a mop: 3.5–4 calories in a minute
Washing floor on hands and knees: 4–4.5 calories in a minute
Sweep a floor: 3.5–4 calories in a minute
Vacuum Carpet: 3.5–4 calories in a minute
Ironing: 2.4 calories in a minute
Carrying over of a basket for linen a ladder march: 3.7 calories in a minute
To wash ware: 2.3 calories in a minute
Groceries unpacking: 3–3.5 calories in a minute

You do not have any justification for stay unusable the moment longer. Start to
BECOME POOR AS YOU CLEAN!

#theoryplushouseworktheory!

It was a little while after I found and saved the above anonymous piece of content that I formulated #theoryplushouseworktheory!

#theoryplushouseworktheory! involves doing a household, care or personal-upkeep task while reading, listening to or watching works relating to theory and theorists that are freely available online, allowing the worker to think as she works.

Here are some of the tasks I attempted, including an evaluation of their relative success or failure:

On 11 March I painted a room with Farrow and Ball's Pavilion Grey while listening to a number of podcasts and video lectures including Lauren Berlant's 'On the Inconvenience of Other People', Jack Halberstam's 'The Queer Art of Failure' and Donna Haraway's keynote at the Fifth Annual Feminist Theory Workshop, in which she spoke about labour and play in her book *The Companion Species Manifesto*.[17]

House painting is an excellent activity for #theoryplushouseworktheory! as the worker is confined to a relatively small space and is engaged in a quiet activity enabling her to listen. If the work of theory is on video, it is even possible to keep half an eye on what is going on onscreen. However, this is not essential as theory lectures are seldom physically dramatic (though some have PowerPoint presentations).

House painting is in fact too successful as a #theoryplushouseworktheory! activity as the lectures and podcasts are likely to finish before the task is completed. It can be inconvenient to climb down a ladder and difficult to switch between lectures or podcasts with paint on your fingers.

On 29 August I listened to Jonathan Rée on Wittgenstein's *Nonsense* while unloading the dishwasher.[18] This is a short activity. I did not record any other activities that accompanied this lecture, but I assume I must have also tidied the kitchen, wiped the surfaces and perhaps done some washing up.

On 30 September I watched a lecture by Rosi Braidotti while making a chorizo and lentil stew from a recipe that had been given to me by my Argentinian friend Fernando, who put the recipe in a tweet that he later erased (all his tweets auto-erase after a month).[19] Cooking is a sporadically satisfying #theoryplushouse-worktheory! companion activity as it involves attention to the recipe, changes of position including frequent turning away from the laptop to fetch ingredients, etc., plus heat and noise. It is also messy, meaning it can be difficult to change or pause podcasts without the interruption of handwashing.

I have mostly utilised #theoryplushouseworktheory! while undertaking substantial cooking enterprises such as making lunch for friends. On this occasion I made the following notes transcribed from Braidotti's lecture:

a) 'The crucial element is shared affinities: what are the ethical passions that pull us, whose suffering, whose pain, did we forget to forget?'

b) 'We are walking around inhabited by the death of others that we are trying to redeem.'

c) 'We are in this together but we are not one, and certainly not the same': stew as social model.

All spring, I walked my ex's dog while listening to Hubert Dreyfus's lectures on Heidegger's *Being and Time*. This was a very good #theoryplushouseworktheory!

exercise, though at the time I was on a limited data plan so was reluctant to stream these un-downloadable lectures often. I also lived in an area with intermittent signal and the lectures would often be interrupted, depending on the route of my walk. Dog walking prevents easy notetaking. Hubert Dreyfus died during one of my dog walks.

From September to December that year I did little or no #theoryplushouseworktheory! as I was working in Paris.

From January to March the next year I did little or no #theoryplushouseworktheory! as I was working in Manchester.

On 14 April I ironed while listening to John David Ebert explain Derrida's *Of Grammatology*.[20] Ironing is a good companion activity for #theoryplushouseworktheory! as it involves little noise and takes place in one room. The ironer is in a fairly static position so can not only hear well but occasionally glance at the screen. The only drawbacks are

a) The screen must be placed at a lower level than the ironing board on a chair—which means I have to incline my head to see it—if I am not to place the screen on the kitchen counter, which also works but means I would face directly into the eye-level kitchen cupboards

and

b) In order to stop the video and go back over a point, it is necessary to put the hot iron down in a safe place on the ironing board then lean over the ironing board to reach my laptop, which can feel a little risky. Ironing is the best regular household task for #theoryplushouseworktheory! and it is the household task I have undertaken most frequently in conjunction with theory study.

A third drawback (c) is that it is a relatively luxurious task: clothes may need to be washed, but do they really need to be ironed? The heap of clothes that can reasonably be said to need ironing either runs out too soon or feels like a waste of time.

On 16 April I watched Brian McGee interview John Searle while I sorted laundry. The task of sorting laundry is too quick and physically involving to be a good companion activity for #theoryplushouseworktheory! To effectively sort laundry, it would be better to listen to an audio-only podcast on Bluetooth headphones while moving freely about the house.

On 3 July I altered a skirt while listening to an interview with Angela Nagle, author of *Kill All Normies*, on SoundCloud.[21] The interview was hosted by @VirtualFutures, an organisation that had invited me to speak at a tech culture conference the week after, at which Nagle would also appear. I was keen to see Nagle at the conference, though I did not agree with a lot of her book. (In the event, I did not attend Nagle's talk as I was too hungover after the conference party the night before.) The skirt was a size too big for me. I had bought it on eBay knowing this and was pleased to find it could easily be altered. I wore the altered skirt to the conference.

Sewing is a fine companion activity for #theoryplushouseworktheory!, suffering only from the necessity of securing with pins then putting down the sewing in order to wind back or pause the podcast, adjust the volume, etc.

Because sewing can be done partially by touch alone it is useful when watching theory on video, though on this occasion Nagle's interview was audio only.

On 30 October I glued a length of Velcro onto a wooden batten to hang a decorative quilt I had bought in a charity shop. I sewed the corresponding piece of Velcro onto the quilt while listening to McKenzie Wark explain her *Hacker Manifesto* on YouTube.[22] I mentioned this on Twitter using her twitter handle plus the #theoryplus-houseworktheory! hashtag. As a result, Wark followed me and I followed her back.

I regard this as a particularly successful instance of #theoryplushouseworktheory! as it not only took in listening to theory and doing housework but involved an encounter with a living theorist. Though I have no need to hang any more quilting, it might be possible to alert other theorists to my project in a similar way during an alternative activity.

On 23 November I read 'Marx and Jargon' by Keston Sutherland online while shaving a wool blanket with a small battery-powered defuzzer. I sat cross-legged on the settee and draped the blanket over my legs. I switched on the defuzzer and applied it to the blanket in the same way I would if I were shaving my legs using an electric shaver, working in circular movements to make sure I covered the entire area.

While doing this (as the shaver blades were safely covered by a mesh screen), I did not look down at my legs but at the text so that, although I could not evaluate how effectively I was removing bobbles from the blanket, I was able to concentrate on my chosen work of theory.

During this session I also looked up Keston Sutherland on Wikipedia where I found that in 2016 he had been 'trapped in a narrow pipe for over thirty-six hours, an experience he described as "like being reborn".'[23]

This instance of #theoryplushouseworktheory! was on the whole effective, both in housework and theoretical terms. Drawbacks included

a) The noise of the shaver, which distracted a little from reading the text.

b) The necessity of pausing every so often to reposition the blanket in order to find a new area to be shaved, or to unblock or empty the shaver.

c) The necessity of not looking down at the blanket while reading the text. To have looked down often would have been to lose the thread of Keston Sutherland's argument; not to look down at all would have restricted my ability to evaluate my effectiveness in shaving the blanket. I could hear a small cutting noise, which I associated with what I imagined might be the sound of an ant biting into a leaf with scissor-like incisors, each time the shaver encountered a wool bobble, so I had some idea of the effectiveness of my work.

d) Like ironing, shaving a blanket is a 'luxury' housework activity and is also (hopefully) a one-time or at least very infrequent task, leaving few future occasions for this activity to be repeated during a #theoryplushouseworktheory! session.

The blanket is a decorative blanket used as a throw, so I could be satisfied that the blanket's appearance was part of its function and that the shaving served or responded to an aspect of the blanket's functionality. The blanket measures approximately 140 × 140 centimetres, so affords a lot of time for listening to, reading or watching theory.

This is the extent of my experiments with #theoryplus-houseworktheory! so far. I have rejected many household tasks as incompatible with the study of theory. I have not yet tried a number of tasks I believe might be suitable to the project. These include: waxing my legs/bikini line, weeding, scrubbing the kitchen tiles and cleaning either bookshelves or kitchen shelves used to store either food or crockery and kitchen implements. Some identical tasks were tried on several occasions though only a single instance of each activity has been recorded here.

Thought Experiment #4: Use

> *The shop seemed to be full of all manner of curious things—but the oddest part of it all was that whenever she looked hard at any shelf, to make out exactly what it had on it, that particular shelf was always quite empty: though the others round it were crowded as full as they could hold.*
>
> —Lewis Carroll, *Through the Looking-Glass*

1.

There's a shop near me called Objects of Use and it's a minimalist shop of handcrafted objects. These objects can be used just as manu-*factured things are, but it takes some time to recognise what some of them could be used for.*[1] *The shop has far more objects in it than a minimalist would use, and its piling up is what makes the objects attractive—its piling up and its neat triage.*

As soon as you have enough to stop worrying, you have enough to worry about stopping. But objects look so good when they're waiting on the shelf, all looking useful, none of them in use, none of them having been used, objects I've never thought of using such as a reindeer-leather coin purse or an Onsen basket. They look good when they're ready for use; better than when being used and better than when they have been used.

The shop is repeated online, where it is divided into sections:

There is, especially, a section of objects called 'work'.

There is, especially, a section of objects called 'person'.

2.

'The intellectual, C. P. Snow believes, is always a luddite,' wrote A. M. Hilton, who coined the term 'cyberculture' in 1963. 'He seeks individuality.'[2] *Opposing 'individuality' to technology, Hilton did not believe that handcrafted objects would persist once manufactured objects had blurred their aesthetic. But Hilton didn't predict the mass-production of 'individuality'.*

Like C. P. Snow, A. M. Hilton sought individuality by using her initials not her name, which screened (non-exclusive OR) her gender or defaulted (XOR, exclusive or*) to male, as in 1963 woman ≠ intellectual. Hilton had no Wikipedia page before 2019 when I caused one to be made, which caused her individuality to be screened, either in the sense of 'overwritten' by the revelation of the gender she chose to hide, or (non-exclusive* OR or *exclusive XOR) in the sense of 'projected' by the revelation of the gender she'd had to disguise.*

And, as for me, no one sees me when I'm being useful offline. There's nothing that can be projected here. Have I been granted a residency in a place from which I can say nothing? If I speak from this place, will it immediately pay back whoever granted me this residency? Or could I overwrite my self online?

Wondering what 'I' can be when I'm not being of use, I am making a self online by collecting virtual objects that self would like to have. But is online anyplace I can be, my onscreen currency—having been a) kind of ok looking and b) hopeful—declining both by duration and by choice?

Any successful self is reproduction: the art of keeping on making a self by hand, even if it is the self.

4 Not Working

Women Working Screens, Like, Forever . . .

> *How can anyone live without that? With a single side, a single face, a single sense. On a single plane. Always on the same side of the looking glass.*
>
> —Luce Irigaray, *This Sex Which Is Not One*

Remember that when a screen is on, we say that it is 'working'.

When I'm not doing work offline, I sit in front of a screen and the screen is working and I am working. We work in the same way in that, although I'm not always working at anything in particular, I am showing signs of life. I am capable of functioning. I am 'on'. When a screen's off, can it (can I?) be said to be working? Am I sleeping? Am I dreaming, like Alice? And which side of the screen is the dream? Perhaps I am on standby, a Heideggerian 'standing reserve' transformed by technology into part of its process. I am perhaps a word processor.

I'm thinking about my place in the precarity economy, for what's art if not enterprise? I'm getting very personal about personal computing, about my Airbnb scores, my eBay scores. When I feel like nothing, I buy something online. Or sell it. Panic in the morning until I can stretch words round the situation of renting my life out to others (the rooms, I mean, their furniture, their family romance), while living on the side to make ends meet. I still feel this 'real' life belongs to me, if only because I sell it.

Online I am working/not working: I am working towards something beyond the work I'm doing. This is the work of self. If any successful online self is repetition, repetition becomes automatic, which is the opposite of autonomy, and self becomes a matter of working through time. If I used all the time available, I could get all the work I have to do in space done in time. If I could get through time quicker, I'd arrive more quickly at the money, though I'd lose my life to get there.

Can I self-make a self that can make screens work for me? Is this making different from the working? Or is this self a Mechanical Turk, only appearing to work at the work I am already doing? Can this process also be productive of a self that is not put to work? And is productivity a good way to evaluate anything?

What I am working towards is self and what I am working with is self, which is simultaneously material and end and process. The screen produces the 'personal' only in seeming opposition to itself. It is a laborious interface where I put my self to work. In the service of what?

On/off. Screens suggest a split. I could coin a word, and perhaps it would have some value in the screen economy. *Spliterity*: a combination of 'alterity' and 'austerity'. The splitting and putting to work of the self as an object, what Heidegger, in 'The Question Concerning Technology', called an 'instrumental self'.[1]

In psychological terms, spliterity can be self-othering: depersonalisation. But any split produces at least two things. And it can be worth something to the human, who is also a worker—a contemporary worker whose personal work is both requested and rewarded in affective terms—to evaluate herself as a thing. The self, as Heidegger's 'standing reserve', is a component of technology-enabled precarity, that nevertheless keeps something in reserve, in play.

Keys Passport Charger Phone

> *'Would you tell me, please, which way I ought to go from here?'*
>
> *'That depends a good deal on where you want to get to.'*
>
> —Lewis Carroll, *Alice's Adventures in Wonderland*

(Spliterity: someone I'd thought was a friend stopped me in the street and told me who I was. He told me this by verifying where I spend my time and for how long; by asking me to confirm where my children spend their time and with whom and also for how long, and also how long I spend with them and where I am when I am not with them. He asked me to repeat these facts back to him aloud, and then asked me how I earn my money. He used the words 'there' and 'here' and other prepositions including 'until', 'after' and 'while'. The facts are nothing to do with where I am at all. He was only being friendly, and a good way to be friendly, he thought, was to captcha my whereabouts. He thought he knew what I was from position and duration. My whereabouts have

nothing to do with where I am at all, because he missed out screens.)

Offline, time is a point in space. 'Personal deixis' is the linguistic prepositionality in which words are understood by their spatial distance from 'I'. Based in the present body, offline deixis is a relational position: under, over, after, before. Wherever 'I' am is always here *and* now.

But, online, space is a point in time, and 'I' exist at a certain uncertain point, where hyperlinks compress space into milliseconds. How fast can I move through screen-space? Travelling without moving, I sit in front of the screen, but I am equally 'on' line: at its beginning, middle and end. A word processor, I feel something move through me. This is a moving experience, and I am moved at affective speed as screen mode is like/heart/star. I am transported.

If I am to be moved, the screen must be something to get across: a barrier, a gap, an interface. The promise of connection relies on the idea of distance. Every screen loneliness is contextualised by the possibility of the collective. Touch a screen and something happens, or appears to. Being in touch is as small a degree of separation as from finger to key.

(To live according to my offline location was to live under a screen. I was screened by my relational position, which screened my relational work, screening others from it and screening me from them. The screen was transparent. I was living behind glass. I could see the people in the street, walk by them, touch them. However close they got, they paid no attention. Wherever I was, my position was

always elsewhere. I could eat with them, talk with them, sleep with them: it didn't matter.)

Onscreen is a flexible orientation. Most people carry one constantly, and those who don't are in constant disorientation from their screen position, which is not just geolocation but an orientation from which work, and the work of self, can be done anytime, which is also anywhere.

Communication technology, wrote media theorist Marshall McLuhan in 1964, creates 'involvement in depth'.[2] Depth implies deixical orientation from the self, mimicking gestalt vision. Gestalt vision is what you get when you're moving. As you pass by, you see the same thing from several angles. It seems to change its position; you seem the still point. I look into my flatscreen. Sitting in front of it, I seem a still point. Nevertheless, it is the only place that allows me to change my position.

'Electric power, equally available in the farmhouse and the Executive Suite, permits any place to be a centre', wrote McLuhan.[3] Time is money, and McLuhan measured speed across space in work: 'Speed-up creates what some economists refer to as a center–margin structure. When this becomes too extensive for the generating and control center, pieces begin to detach themselves and to set up new center–margin systems of their own.'[4]

I don't know how I'd get to a farmhouse from an Executive Suite or vice versa: I've never been in either. I don't know how I'd get there or at what speed, or whether my speed would be electric. I also don't know why. My online work centres have been libraries and coffee shops and pubs. They have been buses and trains and airplanes. They have been parks and playgroups and doctors', dentists', hospitals' and other types of waiting rooms, all structured around a slightly antiquated style of waiting in which not every moment is used for work, which I guess makes them ideal for the kind of work that detaches from the centre–margin structure. I should also mention my table at home and my sofa and all the spaces there that are also not work spaces, as, yes: there is no distinction between my work table and any other table. And, like many women, I also work in bed.

(The man I'd thought a friend was asking regarding
my whereabouts
and I was code-switching
between online and off.
I can't tell you why this made me so angry.)

Like the artist Lily Briscoe in Virginia Woolf's *To the Lighthouse*, whenever I think of work, I see clearly before me a large kitchen table, 'one of those scrubbed board tables, grained and knotted, whose virtue seems to have been laid bare by years of muscular integrity'.[5] I imagine this as what, in furniture stores, is called a 'farmhouse table' (though in the farmhouse it's probably called a 'table'). Not that I have such a table. And, if I did, I wouldn't call what I did at it (or on it) work that has 'muscular integrity'. (At what point does the muscle become integral? Is it at the point of making, or using or maintaining the table after use?) I wouldn't work at making the table, and I wouldn't do other muscular work at the table (what would that be? Kneading something, perhaps?), nor would I lay bare its virtue or mine by dint of muscular scrubbing. There is a countertop in my kitchen made of wood-imitating plastic. And there is a table in the next room for eating at, and also for working.

('Think of a kitchen table, then,' Woolf writes, 'when you're not there.'[6])

I think of the kitchen table when I'm not there. I think of the sort of table that could be in a farmhouse but might look out of place in an Executive Suite (with both its capital letters), in which the kitchen is no more than a cubicle that demonstrates it knows real cooking goes on elsewhere.

Like Woolf's Lily Briscoe, who is an artist, I am instructed to think of the kitchen table *when you're not there* but when the table is. The table—or the idea of a table, or the idea of the idea of a table—is always there, even when I'm not. The table is more there than I am. Lily was instructed to think of the table in order to imagine Mr Ramsey's work, which was philosophical, and might have been about the table being there or not, or was *like* the table but was not muscularly integral to the table.[7] He was not there when the table was being made nor when the table was being used, with either process's muscular integrity. He may have occasionally been served at the kitchen table, but, mostly: how can he have thought of it except without being there?

As I do both paid and relational work at my table, and also eat and do the online work of self, how can I think of not being there? How can I get any perspective?

Philosophers like tables, Sara Ahmed writes in *Queer Phenomenology*. If Ahmed notes the number of tables in philosophy, I would like to note the number of tables in programming. A table that has integrity might be a truth table. A truth table tells you all possible 'truths' given a particular set of inputs: several inputs, one output.

Ahmed wrote that a table is a venue for orientation towards performances of gender and race.[8] For me, to be at the table is an orientation towards various kinds of work. Ahmed sits at the table and argues with her colleagues and relations. When I am not alone at the table, I am in relation, often doing relational work. When I am not with my relations, I am still in relation to the table. The work that is not my work as a relation also takes place at the table, which now supports a small, bright window to elsewhere: a screen. The table has become a platform.

I can sit at the table. I can eat or work at it. I can even dance on it, converting it into a stage. But is it a platform from which I can usefully speak?

Ahmed says the tables can be turned. To turn away from the table, while staying there, is a gesture of complaint and also of desire: a desire to stay at the table, though not on the same terms but in the name nevertheless of the relations a table can support. Ahmed (in her lecture 'Closing the Door: Complaint as Diversity Work') goes on to talk about walls and doors but not about windows. I have used my screen work at the table as a wall that is also a window to alternative deictic relations (why else would my parents ban first books at the table, then screens?). The table may be there in order that the offline 'I' am not.

(If self-writing is a complaint
where can my complaint deictically be addressed?
And to whom?)

Ahmed addresses her complaint to the table while remaining there. A screen allows me to leave the table, without moving, without complaint or even asking, 'May I?' In programming terms, it is less an 'error' that asks to be fixed than a 'mistake' that, undiscovered, may cause the entire program to fail.

(How far is friendship? Sometimes the near are very far away. Then there is screen intimacy. Better keep quiet and, when data is captcha'd, give the wrong details, offer the expected narrative. Keep things trivial, tautologous. Most people do.)

To be asked to justify where I live now is impossible. Having allowed myself to become a location IRL, the screen freed me to expand into its virtual dimensions. Only looking out from the screen allowed me to change my offline deixical position.

The relations between online and off are not fixed orientations. My table has become host to a variety of digital platforms, each allowing, and requiring of me, a different orientation. Each server serves a different purpose, simultaneously asking that I serve them in the name of serving myself: self-service. Still, now the screen works for me, even as it requires me to work myself into something that works for it. Screentime expands the space available to me offline into space I can move across, space that moves me. The difference is affective and effective. Moving or fixed, I'm very used to sitting at a table while being transported.

Simultaneously here and elsewhere, the digital screen promises a new horizon, a gestalt vanishing point at which the aesthetics of production meet the production of aesthetics. Squinting across time into the future, it's possible to infer a space in which a subject may be able to appear.

Thought Experiment #5: Work

(Because people online complain that writing is work.)

A woman sits in front of a screen, which is a logic gate. Each XOR is exclusive: something of her must be excluded. Each OR is non-exclusive, allowing for compromise.

Which is like
the composition of self as writing, each
word a binary gate.

Is writing a self onscreen like the work of kneading meat for meatloaf in Chantal Akerman's film Jeanne Dielman, *work done by its subject, which is also the work of putting work onscreen, done by the real-life actor and filmmaker Delphine Seyrig? Or is it like the work of sewing underwear in an underwear factory in Elfriede Jelinek's novel* Women as Lovers, *which is the work of making work into words done by the writer but not by her subjects, the word-women Paula and Brigitte?*

Is the work of writing a self onscreen like the work of waiting for another word for a novel or the work of waiting for another word for a screenplay? Is it like the work of waiting for the right word for a LinkedIn profile? Is it like the work of waiting for the right word for a dating profile?

Or is writing a self onscreen anything like the work of waiting offscreen? Is it like the work of waiting in a bar, waiting tables in a bar which are also built for waiting, or is it like the work of waiting in a bar, waiting for someone to arrive who does/does not arrive, which is not called work but is done in time bought by work elsewhere, and I guess could be called a date because it is a place but also a time? Both these kinds of waiting work rely on paying and also on paying attention.

In the first kind of work you pay attention in order to be paid and in the second you pay attention in order to pay. And both these kinds of work rely on spending time—as all work is about time—on a gap of space that can be crossed by spending time or a gap of time that can be crossed by attention paid. And both kinds of work rely on time spent on the out-of-hours work of self. These are both kinds of relational work because all waiting work is done in relation, and these are both kinds of work I have done.

Why have I worked in these places? Because they are places it has been easy for me to be placed in, and because I have time to spend. Also, because sometimes, not always, I am paid with money or otherwise in attention paid.

Why work out-of-hours, while doing relational work, on making a self? Because a self is a bounded thing, that does this and not this, rather than an unbounded thing of which anything can be asked or commanded: baggy activities that have no edge, which won't get you far in the work of self?

Because the hardest work I have done is work of waiting that does not rely on the out-of-hours work of self, and this has all been work done offline and without writing. It is work that has no name, done by selves that have no names, only functions. It is work that happens on any day that has no date, though it is also work across time. It is the work of waiting for a bus, if you don't have a car, and the work of waiting to be paid, if you don't have the money. It is the work of waiting in all kinds of waiting room—medical, legal, procedural—which are places built for waiting. It is also the work of waiting when you've worked at all kinds of relational work all day and it's about time someone came, but someone doesn't come. And also the work of having worked at all kinds of relational work all day, but you're waiting for no one to come. These are also all kinds of work I have done.

And of all these kinds of work, the worst kind was the work of waiting for someone who does not come, which meant there was no end to the other kinds of work, and the best kind of work was waiting for no one to come—that, and the work of writing.

What I am writing about is: Where is my workplace? Also, what I am writing about is: Where isn't? Also, I should write about when is my workplace and also what am I working for and who am I working for. Not to mention what am I working on, and is this working for me?

5
Am I those Names?

'This must be the wood,' she said thoughtfully to herself, 'where things have no names. I wonder what'll become of my name when I go in?'

—Lewis Carroll, *Through the Looking-Glass*

I am very tired of using my self as an example, but such is my situation. Each day I wake up thinking I can write something *like* my self onscreen. Each day I think it will be elegant and short, like a tweet: it will be lovely, like Instagram; it will be knowing, like a meme; it will be endless, like a comments thread and like a comments thread, it will trail off and that will be ok.

Thinking I could live onscreen, I threw everything else away. The first thing I got rid of was old names, offline names—relational, material. Also numbers that assigned a value, like dress size or percentage scored, and the names and numbers of buildings and streets and cities that had held me. Having a superfluity of the basest things, depersonalisation was necessarily my methodology.

'People, if you like to believe it, can be made by their names', wrote Gertrude Stein, noting they always have more than one.[1] A housewife—could that be one of mine? People think I don't exist anymore. I am not a modern subject. Yet where else does all the housework go?

'Exploited as you may be, you are not that work,' wrote Silvia Federici: name your occupation and you can knock off at the end of your shift.[2] Could I remake my self through words: an Echo, not even of my own voice but a shared word that alters meaning nonetheless—a name?

The second thing that happened online is everyone got new names, and these names began with @. It was like Adam naming the animals but this time we got to name ourselves. Not that we had free choice—like Judith Butler wrote—but we wore our names with a difference.[3] The first thing we knew from the names was: everyone had a story. Like everyone had a novel inside them and everyone was a star! Everyone had a narrative going on the whole time already, even the people who didn't look like it; the housewives who were 'just housewives' and the just-mothers, the just-cleaners as well as all the women who seemed too young, or too pretty, or too ugly or too old to have been allowed any kind of narrative at all.

Naming is what J. L. Austin called a performative speech act. Names don't just describe, they affect and effect, prescribe and also proscribe. As John Searle wrote in 1989, a 'successful' speech act will 'bring about a fit between words and world'.[4] Names, like other speech acts, are not 'true' or 'untrue', as they can be changed, but their fit with the world can be 'happy' or 'unhappy'. A 'happy' speech act, wrote Austin, is one that fits the world as we can already describe it, according to how the world has been described to us. Renaming, in Austin's offline world, is rare, must be 'correct' and 'complete', and performed by socially sanctioned actors to effect a socially sanctioned state.

Names work differently online, where naming is key. It can lock or unlock. Type in a name. It is a password, a word that allows passing. The name doesn't have to be your name, it just has to be a name that you have right now. A nom-de-script; how easily it can be borrowed.[5] I could call it a mode of address, like an address in a street or an address in programming, a location from which something can be 'called'. Online, a name is called at the point of challenge, as in a fairy tale: 'Speak, friend, and enter.'[6] In cybersecurity, to call all known names is called a brute force attack: RUN!

Here are some names that, when run, are known to unlock; some names and their shadows, pass words:

Name/password
admin/password
test/password
root/master
root/apache
root/unix
root/redhat
danny/danny
sharon/sharon
aron/aron
alex/alex
brett/brett
mike/mike
alan/alan
data/data
http/http
httpd/httpd
traveler/traveler

alice/alice
nobody/nobody
girl/girl[7]

Open Sesame!

To screen is to test for authenticity, as though enough passwords could call into existence some kind of authentic subject. But authenticity is not the screen standard. If spliterity divides the self by function into identifiable iterations, iterability, says Derrida, related to the Sanskrit for 'other', ties 'repetition to alterity'.[8] Like when someone can say 'It me' for about the length of a gif and call it a meme. 'Meme' means 'like' as in 'similar to' and is derived from 'mimetic', which comes from *mimeme*, the Ancient Greek for 'imitated thing'.[9]

We like the meme's likeness to what it is like. It is not identical but an iteration that might be surprising or funny or ironic or similar-but-dissimilar, though always a bit like, and, as an 'imitated thing', it is also something to imitate: an example.

Screen liking is usually binary: an on/off switch. Onscreen, I can't sort of like something. I have to sort it, like it or not. I can unlike something, and if so, I must be unlike it. To be 'unlike' is not to like anything. But to meme is not to 'like' (RTs are not endorsements). Memes replace emotional content: they allow me to like not quite liking, not being quite like. A meme can only continue to exist through ironic re-iteration; it shrugs off iteration that is not also critique but survives via recognisable iterations of form. It prompts reproduction only via modulation.

Memed irony plays not on linguistic elegance but

'failure': the more clunky its iteration (within the limits of recognition of its relationship to the original), the stickier the meme. Offline, irony can be indicated by tone. Online, the live quality of ironic delivery, diluted by distances of space, time, culture and duration, is replaced by a visual indicator: winkyface ;-).

Poe's Law, a description of the codification of onscreen 'irony', works just the same as Epimenides' paradox about offline liars: all winkyfaces imply irony.[10] I am winkyfacing to tell you ironically that I am being ironic. Poe's Law is an autological concept: it does what it describes. Whether 'Poe' (who has never been identified beyond his screen name) was being ironic (and undecidability is irony's crucial component) when he stated, 'Without a winking smiley or other blatant display of humour, it is utterly impossible to parody a Creationist in such a way that someone won't mistake for the genuine article', has also never been decided.[11]

A memed iteration is what Austin called an 'etiolated' speech act, whose clunkiness points up awareness of citation, diluting an audience's understanding of 'intention', which is Austin's proof of a single speaking subject. Such speech acts, he writes, are not only 'ill' but 'infect all utterances' and are 'parasitic'.[12]

Biological evolution is reproduction × modification (the word 'meme' itself a meme, a modulation on 'mimesis', coined by Richard Dawkins in his 1976 book *The Selfish Gene*). But a meme does not have the 'code script' of DNA. Its process is chaotic, its telos not to modulate to survive but to survive in order to modulate: it is Austin's parasite. Its users are (electively, temporarily, for lolz) not its species but its host.

Could I re-name my self ironically? Could I use a name

to reorient my self from the socially reproductive functions of physical reproduction and change my function to *fun*? Could I meme the examples available to me: the female interfaces as seen onscreen, the girls online, the influencers, bloggers, vloggers, who exist because I like them, not being quite like them? Once I have identified them, how should I identify myself with them? And, if my object becomes to self-objectify, what objectives could that serve?

'Sometimes', wrote Judith Butler, 'calling a group of people on the street a "revolution" contributes to the effect of bringing about what it names.'[13]

But sometimes it has the effect of bringing about only what it names.

PART II

GIRL ONLINE / ALICE THROUGH THE LOOKING GLASS

6
Girl Online

Hello, World!

> *Alice tried to fancy to herself what such an extraordinary ways of living would be like, but it puzzled her too much.*
>
> —Lewis Carroll, *Through the Looking-Glass*

'Hello, World!' is the first executable run prompt for any programming language. Blinking into existence, is it a newborn, or an alien? It looks out at you from the screen: it, not you, says, 'Hi!'

What Purpose Did I Serve in Your Life?: in 2013, Marie Calloway, a girl who never grew up, published her only book, a quasi-fictional study of her online selves, whose title flips her first-person narrator into the object role. Using communication technology, 'one is threatened "with the possibility of becoming no more than a thing in the world of the other"' (Avital Ronell quotes R. D. Laing).[1]

'Hello,' says Marie Calloway in the first line of her book's best-known story, 'Adrien Brody'.[2] The lightly fictionalised editor who slept with her, cheating on his girlfriend, is said to be someone I've worked for. A friend, who also worked for him, told me *everyone* knew. At the time Marie Calloway wrote 'Adrien Brody', I was no one. At the time, my friend, then an aspiring author and grad student in New York, was almost someone in that world. At the time, she was watching box sets of an early-2000s TV show called *Sex and the City*, about an aspiring author who made a living writing about her sexual experiences. In *SATC*, my friend saw a model to orient herself towards, an onscreen example with enough to identify with, enough to envy, to produce a movement of desire.

At the time I—a provincial mother in another country that was not New York—was watching *Sex and the City* because it showed me something I could not aspire to. For my friend, it seemed almost real; for me, it was fiction. But we both 'identified' with what we saw onscreen. Why?

The writer and critic Emily Gould called Calloway's story 'Adrien Brody' a 'post, before it became "fiction"'.[3] She means a blogpost (this was 2011) on a blog, short for 'weblog'. Social 'forums' came first, but blogs took a step back from Arendt's public space and were the first entirely personal, self-administered sites.

Text based (as the capacity to produce images remained, at first, limited) and imitating the one-way street of older media, blogs were often (or were often assumed to be) diaries, written under the sign of what Eve Kosofsky Sedgwick calls the 'nonce taxonomy' of gossip: the form used by 'effeminate and gay men, with all women, to have to do not even so much with the transmission of necessary news as with the refinement of necessary skills for making, testing, and using unrationalized and provisional hypotheses about what kinds of people there are to be found in one's world'.[4]

Emily Gould was famous at the time for the diary-style critical columns she published in her eponymous blog *Emily Magazine*. 'Emily Gould' is Emily Gould's IRL name. 'Marie Calloway' is not Marie Calloway's IRL name: her offline name remains a mystery. Carrie Bradshaw, a writer of self-revelatory columns in a pre-blog New York newspaper, may be no one's name IRL, but is the fictional heroine of *Sex and the City*, a US 'comedy-drama' (IMDB) screened between 1998 and 2004, based on a novel written by Candace Bushnell, starring four women, and 'created' by the 'openly gay' (Wikipedia) man Darren Star, whose sexual identity, according to Sedgwick, may signal familiarity with a shared taxonomy.[5] In the show, Carrie appears onscreen writing onscreen and we see her, often late at night, gaze at her words as they appear one by one, glowing on the screen in front of her.

A decade after Carrie's fictional diaries, Calloway's blend of the real and the invented was greeted critically with fascinated disgust. Both works were written during a key moment in self-writing: as the TV's small screen shrank into the even smaller screen of the laptop. Nearly a decade after the publication of Calloway's book, this interplay of storytelling and 'true' personal reflection is taken entirely for granted.

('Reflection' is the ability of a program to read and modify its own structure and behaviour as it runs. 'In this sort of sense, a machine can undoubtably be its own subject matter', wrote Alan Turing.[6])

Both Calloway and Carrie's words cross between old and new media. In *SATC*, Carrie is shown writing on a laptop for a print publication; Calloway writes about and in the language of the internet and is published both online and in print. Both works are set in the imaginary city of New York, which I believe I have visited several times. In the opening credits of the TV show *Sex and the City*, the heroine, Carrie Bradshaw, is in New York City. We first see Carrie's face, looking from side to side, like Rae Armantrout in her poem 'The Pretext', performing her own trans-fiction as she watches Marilyn Monroe 'pretend to pretend to be transfixed'.[7] Then </cut> to sharp, reflective New York City skyscrapers. Then Carrie is walking down a street, and then we switch to a perspective from a moving vehicle crossing the (Brooklyn?) bridge. A tyre splashes </cut>, the water hits Carrie. Carrie (and the action, which has until now been continuously mobile) halts, then </cut> to a bus driving past with an ad for her own newspaper column: 'Carrie Bradshaw knows good sex'.

But she does not, at first, know herself. Is this a moment of miss-recognition in which Carrie confuses her own objectified image with her objective? Over the bus ad's assertion of her authorship, the screen floats the words 'created by darren star'. The creator's name is also the name of the fictional paper, the *New York Star*, that publishes Carrie's words.

(Can we prove any truths about our own structure?
Any diary is Gesamtkunstwerk—
a work of art that talks about itself—just as
any autological word describes itself. A sentence
that does this is an autogram, like:

'This sentence has got forty-four characters.'
As in programming, what isn't there—the gaps—
are also characters.)

Carrie shares more than trans-fiction with Marilyn Monroe. She appears via the girl tropes of rom-com heroines, beauties threatened by their own exorbitance: sometimes mental (Sedgwick on Monroe: 'People can't resist the incandescence of her being so unstable'), sometimes physical ('Like Jello on springs', Jack Lemmon marvels at Monroe's ass bouncing above her high heels, in *Some Like It Hot*).[8] As does Calloway: at the beginning of 'Adrien Brody', 'Marie' trips in heels at the moment she meets her internet crush 'Adrien', who she's only previously met on digital platforms, pointing up her unsteady subject position—a rom-com staple.

In an unscreened take for the *SATC* credits, Carrie is destabilised, not by her image but by her shoes: 'There were two wardrobes. One was the tutu, and we did one pass where Sarah Jessica was wearing a blue dress and didn't get splashed; instead, she trips when she sees the ad.'[9] In the alternate version, Carrie is not sullied by her own image as professional dirt-disher but saved by it. In the smart blue dress, not the kooky pink tutu, she looks less vulnerable. She trips, then noticing her photo, recovers and walks away smiling (at her success? At the irony of her situation in which she is creator, star and audience?).

(Carrie runs; Carrie pauses. Does she halt?
Reflection, in computing, is a halting problem.
It's about knowing when to stop, in order to go on.
While (true) 'continue' does not halt but runs

forever in an infinite loop. On the other hand, the program
Print: Hello, World!
does halt.)

In romantic comedy, beginnings are important because the endings are all the same. But each *SATC* episode ends with a question. Vulture.com states that Carrie asks ninety-two questions throughout the series, although there are ninety-four episodes.[10] It is the question that halts the action.

(Halting is a matter of autonomy: a Turing-complete machine can perform any possible computation. A universal Turing machine can emulate any machine that speaks its language (it is 'Turing-complete'). But a universal Turing machine that halts cannot 'decide' for sure whether the Turing-complete machine it runs will halt or run forever, so the emulation is incomplete. The halting problem remains 'undecidable'.)

Calloway's questions are what the poet and critic Denise Riley calls 'catastrophic': *Do you think I'm pretty? Do you love me?* Calloway's critique embedded in a deadpan representation of her avatar questioning an opaque, online partner. But Carrie's questions are not Calloway's; they are addressed to no one. Or to the viewer. Or the screen. Or herself. Carrie 'wonders' or 'can't help but wonder'; she represents a juxtaposition as ironic as that of being splashed by a bus bearing a perfect image of herself and responds with a question that reflects on its own process: she is *pretending to pretend to be transfixed*.

(Remember, the Turing machine, like Carrie's question, is a thought experiment.)

What does a rhetorical question screen when it is screened? I can't help but wonder, Does this wondering queer the question form, which might be unacceptable if posed so directly as to bring things to a halt, or does it keep the question looping in abeyance?

Symposium and the City

> *Who in the world am I? Ah, that's the great puzzle!*
> —Lewis Carroll, *Alice's Adventures in Wonderland*

> *I was coming from my own home at Phalerum to the city, and one of my acquaintance, who had caught a sight of me from behind, calling out playfully in the distance, said . . . is not the road to Athens just made for conversation? And so we walked, and talked of the discourses on love.*
> —Plato, *The Symposium*

In a famous old book, a group of friends gathers for brunch (with cocktails!), among them a lawyer, a writer and other urban professionals. They are all 'career-oriented, sexually free, and always about putting themselves and their friendship with each other first', but all they want to talk about is love.[11] I'm talking about Plato's *Symposium*.

Like Carrie, the gathered brunchers can't help but wonder:

> *Are men in their twenties the new designer drug? . . . I couldn't help but wonder, what do they*

> *see in us?*[12] (Phaedrus quotes Carrie, season one, episode four.)
>
> *If we can take the best of the other sex and make it our own, has the opposite sex become obsolete?*[13] (Pausanias quotes Carrie, season three, episode four.)
>
> *When did being alone become the modern-day equivalent of being a leper?*[14] (Eryximachus quotes Carrie, season 2, episode 4.)
>
> *Are men just women with balls?*[15] (Aristophanes quotes Carrie, season four, episode ten.)
>
> *Are New Yorkers evolving past relationships?*[16] (Socrates quotes Carrie, season two, episode eleven.)
>
> *If models could cause otherwise rational individuals to crumble in their presence, exactly how powerful was beauty?*[17] (Alcibaides quotes Carrie, season one, episode two.)

This wondering is a rhetorical device called an aporia: an artfully performative, 'etiolated' speech act. It pretends to come naturally out of the speaker's own confusion (I couldn't help but wonder . . .). 'You are a perplexed man', said Meno to Socrates, 'and reduce others to perplexity.'[18]

('Perplexity per word' is a measure of how well an AI can use a dataset to produce a predictive text that can, for example, as in Turing's test, convince you it's a woman.)

Like Alice in Wonderland, Carrie not only asks the questions but, embodying each dilemma, is 'in question'. And I can't help but wonder, Does Carrie, like Alice, never learn? Or perhaps the performance of the question is the point.

(If the halting problem is a question of not being able to decide, 'autoepistemic' logic allows a program to reflect on its process. In logic programming, certainty ranges from zero to one. To retrieve an answer, autoepistemeic logic allows a system to infer plausibly from a range of possibilities, even when the user is not asking exactly the right question.)

'Power speaks here in this moment of hesitation,' writes Sara Ahmed. 'To create awkwardness is to be read as being awkward', which can be a species of diversity work.[19] A body can choose to behave in a way that maintains the status quo (to her own detriment) or she can openly flout it, but this hesitation, like Carrie's halting in front of her own image, is a gesture that produces a moment of choice. Or alternatively, marks the spot where a choice might, or should, be.

(The autoepistemic programming language Planner converts a failure to find the answer to a question into an answer:

if [*not (goal* p*)*], then [*assert* ¬p].*)*

Aporia might express what the critic Lauren Berlant calls 'impasse', an inchoate and pressingly political 'situation' in which we stop and can't help but wonder, What if the objects we've been given (and the objectives we've been given) in no way fit our world? It prompts a detour from the polis into what Berlant calls 'juxtapolitical' territory that works to organise life 'without threading through dominant political institutions'.[20] This is good news and bad news for any minority subject who might desire a place at the table but whose exclusion (while they are serving or even sitting at it) renders them glitchily present and absent simultaneously, an undecidable question.

('Paraconsistent' logic is inconsistency tolerant, allowing self-referential statements and reasoning with inconsistent information, without detouring into the trivial in which all statements [speech acts] are equally 'true'. It allows an answer to an undecidable question.)

In the fourth century BC, Pyrrhonist philosophers intentionally posed aporia to themselves and each other in order to produce ataraxia. Ataraxia is not quite euphoria (well-being) but being ok with being only kind of ok. Maybe I can live with that.

(The difficulty with a self-referential or autological statement in computing or natural language can be that, in order to refer to itself, it must contain a framing structure—a word, a statement or an additional number. This creates an 'object' composed of data + behaviour—a genre.)

The 'problem with reifying the status quo', writes Eve Kosofsky Sedgwick, 'is what it does to the middle ranges of agency. One's relation to what is risks becoming reactive and bifurcated, that of the consumer.' The insistence on a yes XOR no answer, run or halt, limits options, especially when 'it is only the middle ranges of agency that offer space for conceptual creativity and change'.[21] These are the ranges of the trivial (self-similar), the aporetic, of narrative that is neither fiction nor 'non'.

'I Confess'

'And the moral of that is— "Be what you would seem to be"—or if you'd like it put more simply—"Never imagine yourself not to be otherwise than what it might appear to others that what you were or might have been was not otherwise than what you had been would have appeared to them to be otherwise."'

—Lewis Carroll, *Alice's Adventures in Wonderland*

I confess that, beginning to write online, feeling little agency myself, I sought a (literary) agent. Should I write a book? And what sort? *You write about cities*, she said, *and love. You should write chick lit.* This was in the late 2000s, the era of the blog-novel: the 'real' as 'fiction'. A woman had just made a fortune turning her blog into a book and so, said the agent, that is what I should write. Looking for examples, I should not read Augustine's *Confessions* or Montaigne's *Essais*; I should read a blogger who called herself 'Petite Anglaise'.

Seeking, like Carrie, to recognise myself in something outside myself, I looked up the blog. If chick lit was cute, this was not cute. It was brutal. The feelings were terrifying: a single mother abroad, diary entries at four a.m., despair couched as cheerily as it could be written, romcom style peeling off raw content. It did not only splash itself with its own reflection; it nearly drowned in it. I read and I was horrified: had what Chris Kraus called the *roman à clef*—the 'thinly veiled story of Me'—got mixed up with the *Story of O*?[22]

On the cover of the novel is Catherine Sanderson's blog name, *Petite Anglaise*, which is also the book's title, and below it her name IRL, splitting her into writer and subject; then, in smaller letters, the words, 'A True Story'. The reviewers on Amazon do not evaluate Sanderson's writing but her self—'I really disliked Catherine and thus, I really can't say I enjoyed the book'—just as the critical reviewers on IMDB do not like the fictional *Sex and the City* because they do not like the characters' morals and they do not like the characters personally.[23] (They also complain that the women's lives and finances are 'unrealistic', and many prefer *The Sopranos*, another HBO show of the same era about male mafiosos whose glamorous lifestyles are the fruit of extortion and murder.)

The reviewers do not like that Sanderson's was a 'true story'. They would, they say, have preferred fiction. She is not a 'real writer' because she draws too much on real life. They know it's her life because it's on her blog, and blogs are 'real'. They suspect each unpleasant or morally questionable incident to have taken place in the life of the author exactly as it is written in the novel, and to splash back on her. They expected something 'lighter' and Sanderson's book makes them uncomfortable. It is 'not chick lit', they complain.

This may be 'complaint as diversity work'.[24] Halted by the recognition of the woman who is splashed by the dirt of her own image, the reader is forced to think not only, *What if that really happened?* but, *If so, how do I feel about knowing it did?* This not only 'tolls the knell of genealogy or of genericity' (Derrida) but busts the division between art and ethics, offline and on, 'reality' and 'fiction'.[25]

At the point of deciding *Petite Anglaise*'s genre, Amazon readers are faced with a textual aporia—a transfixing question posed by someone pretending to pretend to be perplexed—and their complaints and defences are impassioned. A work in a new genre that could be called the 'blog-novel', *Petite Anglaise* admits its relation to life. So its readers do not complain about *how* Sanderson writes. They complain about single mothers, or complain about the way single mothers are treated; complain about women who have casual sex or about men who exploit them; complain about, or defend, the way women treat their friends, their husbands, their children, their colleagues; complain about the way women treat themselves.

'The effect of the medium is made strong and intense just because it is given another medium as "content" . . . The book is a private confessional form that provides a "point of view". The press is a group confessional form that provides communal participation': that was McLuhan, writing in the 1960s.[26] Update: the diary used to be a private form. Then it became 'press', but only just: part of the semi-amateur First-Person Industrial Complex that paid mostly women writers mostly very little—and sometimes nothing at all—for everything they'd got.[27]

The diary used to be for thoughts that were unspeakable. The blog made it about sharing them with as many people as possible. The digital diary put onscreen the screened-off 'private' self. Good. Privacy was seldom good for women. In its name, it has been (it is) the location of crimes committed against them. Private is often not 'private for women' but 'women being private for others'. The control of women's privacy has too seldom been in their hands, and 'private life' has sometimes meant that women were private property. Carrie, Calloway and Sanderson/'Petite'—characters of different and mixed levels of fictionality, using different genres among the girl genres known as 'genre'—claimed their diaries as their own private property. And sold them.

A girl's diary is a think (*sic*, autocorrect) with an artificial lock, which points up that it has an inside and an outside, but that's all show. You can break into it easily (if leaving evidence). A 'girl' is free to refuse the gift of a diary with its heart-shaped lock but she may find no other paper to write on. Why give diaries to girls, not boys? A girl must be somewhere secrets are kept. But a girl who keeps a diary is also assumed to be innocent, so what secrets could she write? A kept woman is paid for her privacy. Sanderson (like Calloway, Carrie) kept a diary, and then it kept her.[28] It was an account of herself that was entered in her end-of-year accounts. And I can't help but wonder,

How can a girl give an account of herself in all innocence?

And:

What happens when the personal, the private, the amateur, insists it is work?

So, what's the story with the blog-novel? Readers' opprobrium (or admiration) relies not only on their knowing the story of *Petite Anglaise* is 'real' but on their knowing the real framing story of the blogger's lucrative sale of her 'life' as work. The dream Sanderson's readers were buying was not only, or even primarily, that of being the 'Catherine' in her book but the dream of being an amateur 'non-writer' who beats the system of girl-privacy (including the notion that 'female' acts—sex, relationships, care, motherhood—are outside the realm of capital) and monetizes her life through genre.[29]

An eye looks out from the header of the *Petite Anglaise* blog. It shows on the page tab, too—sophisticated design for 2009. Sanderson is looking out at us watching her looking.

The Old Girl Who Lived in Her Shoes

> *'I must be kind to them,' thought Alice, 'or perhaps they won't walk the way I want to go! Let me see: I'll give them a new pair of boots every Christmas.'*
>
> —Lewis Carroll, *Alice's Adventures in Wonderland*

'In New York, you're always looking for a job, a boyfriend or an apartment.' Carrie's trilemma echoes one found in Armistead Maupin's similarly titled *Tales of the City*—another novel turned TV comedy-drama with a female protagonist, 'created' by an 'openly gay' man: 'You can have a hot lover, a hot job and a hot apartment, but you can't have all three at the same time.'[30] Not to mention the programmers' trilemma: you can have good, cheap and fast, but you can only pick two. In one episode of *SATC*, Carrie cannot pay her deposit on a 'good apartment' because she spends all her money on shoes.

In *The Origin of the Work of Art*, Martin Heidegger fixes on Van Gogh's drawing of a pair of shoes (which Heidegger believes are the work shoes of a peasant woman but, as the artist made several studies of similar shoes at different times, may well have been his own) as a paradigm for 'thingness' that disappears into use, becoming 'equipment' (for all that, what Heidegger examines is a work of representation, which has another use altogether).[31]

(In mathematical logic, a 'system' or 'formal theory'—like set theory, the basis of logic gates—is a series of axioms from which other theorems can be derived. Any such system prompts a programmers' trilemma: it may contain 'completeness', 'consistency' and 'effective axiomatisation' ['computability' or Turing-completeness], but the necessary 'incompleteness' of any system containing enough arithmetic means that, like Carrie, it can't have all three at the same time.)

'Cruel optimism', writes Lauren Berlant, in their book of that name, 'exists when something you desire is actually an obstacle to your flourishing.'[32] Carrie desires a boyfriend, job and apartment: all three at the same time. She also desires shoes, which are an easier short-term objective. Because she reorients her desire to shoes, we are free to critique that desire as we simultaneously indulge our own desire for these objects, not to mention our (and Carrie's) desire for the vicarious glamour of desiring, aka window shopping.

Stilettos (Carrie's shoe of choice) do not only *not* disappear with use into being 'equipment', they become more visible.[33] They are conspicuous consumption plus conspicuous leisure; they say, 'I am not "useful"', as well as, 'My owner has enough money not to be "useful" either.' Their 'use' cannot be seen; what can be seen is their *uselessness*. Nevertheless, Carrie's shoes are very useful for the task of self-presentation, which is how she makes her money.

Though she works to pay for them, they are also her work clothes, her tools, her equipment. They help her to fulfil her function, which is to look like she has no function. As she uses them, not only do they become more visible, they blot out her appearance otherwise. At a second remove—on the TV or digital screen, or the cover of a chick lit novel—a pair of stilettos says nothing about their owner's race, age, gender or body, only the owner's ability to afford them, and what's more, as representations, they allow participation in the cultures they conjure not for the price of a pair of Manolos but for a paperback or a Netflix subscription.

('Completeness' means all questions can be answered 'yes' or 'no'. 'Incompleteness' means some statements, like the halting problem, are not provable within the system. Kurt Gödel's 1931 incompleteness theorem is designed to reflect not only on other systems but on itself. It can't help but wonder about its own incompleteness [impredicativity].)

'Genre as defence', writes Berlant, may provide 'fantasy as a life-sustaining defence against the attritions of ordinary violent history'.[34] It can operate through 'absorption in pretty things'.[35] Carrie is absorbed both in classifying her objects of desire, and in coming to possess them. Both are acts of self-definition, providing (a pair of) platforms from which to speak. But Carrie is not self-possessed. Her values are all wrong. She chooses to desire things that are 'trivial', things that make her more 'self-similar' to her image on the bus ad: 'successful' self as repetition. She pays no attention to the demands of 'real life'.

This is why *SATC* annoys people. It is what Kristeva called 'exorbitant': too much money for too many shoes. At the same time, it is not enough. The viewer, or reader, is prompted to feel strongly about something s/he must also acknowledge is 'trivial' in its excess. The experience chick lit conjures in the reader—when it is not the wholehearted suspension of generic sorting (the immersive 'beach read')—is annoyance. The 'shock of the new' is replaced by the 'annoyance of the cute', whose push-pull produces a 'trivial' feedback loop, providing no moment of transcendence but providing something.

(In logic terms, trivial 'identifies what should not be identified and is undesirable from a logical point of view because it identifies what is not identical, namely, truth and falsehood'.[36]*)*

A genre that exists by virtue of its reader demographic's IRL gender and economic precarity—unlikely to have as good an apartment, boyfriend (if 'good' means economically successful) or job as Carrie, or even a pair of Manolos—it offers a blatantly 'unreal' escape route.

(Gödel's theorem is in the field of mathematical logic, but it is also a problem of computability. An 'undecidable' problem is uncomputable: no algorithm exists to answer 'yes' or 'no'. The halting problem is a decision problem. A Turing machine is necessarily incomplete: it cannot have a hot lover, a hot job and a hot apartment. It cannot solve the halting problem, which remains 'undecidable'. An undecidable answer is also called 'independent'. A decidable problem depends on its own recursiveness, its ability to call itself from within its own code. A semi-decidable

problem may run forever if the answer is 'yes' but halt if the answer is 'no'.)

I am sometimes told that I am 'trivial' for paying attention to *Sex and the City*, that I should feel guilty about watching the privileged characters whose lives are unlike mine, as though to orient myself towards the screen were to identify completely, to desire their objects or to share their objectives. But to refuse to pay attention to the 'trivial' is to refuse to pay attention to the feedback loop of most people's lives—or to people's lives most of the time—or to understand 'genre as defence'.

SATC asks some very good questions, like: 'What does it mean to want a sense of something rather than something?' (Lauren Berlant can't help but wonder).[37] A 'sense' of something does not satisfy the senses as a real pair of Manolos would, but nor does it ever degrade into 'equipment', as even Carrie's shoes will. And I can't help but wonder if it isn't useful for watchers of *SATC* to participate in this onscreen thought experiment in the virtual pursuit of something that is 'actually an obstacle to your flourishing'.

(A universal Turing machine is a thought experiment in desire and identification. A universal Turing machine can emulate any machine that it is not. A universal Turing machine that halts can run a version of a Turing machine that never halts.)

Drag Diary

> *'I can't explain myself, I'm afraid, sir,' said Alice, 'because I'm not myself, you see.'*
>
> —Lewis Carroll, *Alice's Adventures in Wonderland*

The blog might be called 'waste prose', like Lichtenberg's *The Waste Books*, which were *essais* in Montaigne's sense, or in Adorno's *The Essay as Form*: 'useless', incomplete, diaristic, aphoristic, future and past-facing, privileging its objects (its material) over its objectives, converting data plus behaviour into prose objects, white elephants, bibelots, whatnots, *things*.

And I can't help but wonder, Is the blog the essay form . . . for girls?

Theodor Adorno, in *The Essay as Form*, complains about what conversion to the genre novel does to what he calls 'naïve' personal forms: 'Fictionalised biographies and all the related commercial writing that depend on them are not mere products of degeneration: they are a permanent temptation for a form whose suspiciousness of false profundity does not protect it from turning into slick superficiality.'[38] There is nothing naïve—and therefore valuable—for him about the blog-novel, dependent as it is on the 'defensive' capacities of genre (Berlant). Adorno is suffering from a need to impose firm borders of genre, not realising, as Butler writes, 'that designation supposed to be most in the raw, proves to be always already "cooked".'[39] Or, as Carrie greets us in episode one, season one of *SATC*, 'Welcome to the age of un-innocence,' referencing Edith Wharton, the original New York City girl.

Everyone wants a theory to account for the girl—hardly noticing that girl genres embed self-reflection: the

French collective Tiqqun wrote a whole book of *Preliminary Materials for a Theory of the Young-Girl*, the artist Audrey Wollen coined the term 'sad girl theory', and I must confess that, in a newspaper piece, I called Chris Kraus's autofictional writings 'slapstick tragedy'.[40] Tiqqun, those cowards with no names, frame the Young-Girl in 'critical' language so very unlike the words of the Young-Girl herself. But, in her novel *I Love Dick*, Kraus's formulation of 'lonely-girl phenomenology' is itself a performance of girl-rhetoric relying, like the plot turns of *Sex and the City*, on a dialectic of cute/smart 'And just like that . . .' switchback moves. Only the Young-Girl practitioner dares to inhabit her own language—a mimesis, a meme, a performance of what she already is.

Why does no one take her at her word?

Girl identity is established via word-based personal revelations whose confessional tone relies, like the blog, on a shared understanding of what is 'private'. As Chris Kraus wrote of her avatar's new acquaintance in another autofiction *Aliens and Anorexia*, 'because both of us were girls, Gudrun Sheidecker told me everything about her life'.[41] Lauren Berlant, writing about Mary Gaitskill's novel *Two Girls, Fat and Thin*, calls this process 'trauma talk'.

'Trauma talk', said the poet Vahni Capildeo,

> just sounds violent or distorted, or gabbling, which is like what happens when someone wants to report a rape. They can't tell you, 'Well at six o'clock this happened,' then 'At eight o'clock this happened,' then, 'At eight o'clock the next day I thought this and I felt that so at nine o'clock I rang you'. If they don't present a sort of linear narrative they often get punished because the amount of violence and fragmentation they convey

> is something that doesn't fit in people's idea of a fluent witness.[42]

How can a girl self-represent except via performances of abjection or excess?

The performance of 'girl' identities via girl genres offers the power to both mobilise 'trauma talk' and render it 'readable' without encountering the 'punishment' Capildeo mentions but, at the same time, marginalises these accounts as 'genre'. In this they resemble Michel Foucault's description of the confessional form as entailing the speaker's association with what [he] also wishes to distance [him]self from at the moment of uttering.

Confession is such a drag . . .

Its performative acts of gender melancholy—produced by the push-pull of identification, aspiration, shame and failure inbuilt in both gender (Butler) and confession (Foucault)—mean I can't help but wonder, Is the blog-novel the diary in drag?

Drag recasts two genres of being, in a process akin to Margaret Mead's definition of 'second-order cybernetics', defining them as in no way exclusionary but codependent (in Mead's case: human and nonhuman). Heinz von Foerster added that in second-order cybernetics, the 'observed' system of the first-order becomes an 'observing system', recursive and autopoetic (in the sense of autopoiesis).[43]

Gaitskill's 'girls' are 'overwhelmed by a compulsion to historicise, to narrate their lives to each other, and yet the exchange of personal narrative does not necessarily amount to an intimate exchange of something personal' (Berlant). Each 'girl' functions 'as a formal point of attachment, an opening toward something beyond individuality'. Confession, Foucault adds, is 'one of the main rituals we rely on for the production of truth'.[44]

Like confession, drag's double appearance produces two 'truths' (allowed by paraconsistent logic). As Butler notes, 'Both claims to truth contradict one another and so displace the entire enactment of gender significations from the discourse of truth and falsity.'[45] To be 'thoroughly and radically incredible' is what Butler wishes from gender acts.[46] 'Incredible' puns 'not believable' with 'great'. As in Austin's speech acts, there is no true/untrue here. There are happy and unhappy speech acts, but the diary blog reclaims the excluded middle: it is melancholy.

The novel *Petite Anglaise* insists that its genre is not tragedy but comedy. Butler's gender melancholy offers 'an insight into heterosexuality as both a compulsory system and an intrinsic comedy, a constant parody of itself' that allows a standpoint outside the heterosexual 'self', however seemingly straight its content.[47] Constrained to comic expression, the girl-blog's conversion to the genre novel produces a Butlerian comedy of gender where, tripping in high heels, no girl quite hits the mark. It points up how bodies can never successfully inhabit their names: 'Finding a suitable name to describe the man in my life', wrote Sanderson (no, I think it was 'Petite'), 'is proving almost as difficult as finding a name I approve of to refer to certain parts of my anatomy.'[48]

'With hindsight', writes Sanderson, 'personal blogging lost much of its attraction for me when I could no longer hide behind a pseudonym, and although after the ink was dry on the book deal I felt obligated to continue updating my blog until the books had made it onto the supermarket shelves, my heart was no longer in it.'[49]

In blogs, autofiction and other autotelic enterprises, subject and object, writer and material are one, meaning that for an automatic Alice who continues to trip without ever walking away, it can be difficult to leave the scene of the crime. What is more terrifying than comedy?

'These days', Sanderson wrote in 2013, 'I have very little internet presence.'[50]

The Wikipedia page on 'blog' hardly mentions personal blogging or the experiments in identity it facilitated; it mentions only blogs that dealt with subjects that could already be categorised as nontrivial within the polis (politics, sport, comedy), monologues that already had offline platforms.

And I can't help but wonder, if comedy is tragedy plus time, and if melancholy is characteristic of gender performance, does the durational act of gender melancholy in girl-blogging shade into the feedback loop of Freudian melancholia, becoming not only a reflection but a performative speech act, a primary experience, an inescapable way of being.

And I can't help but wonder, *Is this why girls keep diaries, and women don't?*

And also, *What does a 'girl' gain by refusing to call herself a woman?*

The Oldest Girl in the World

> *'Shall I never get any older than I am now? That'll be a comfort, one way—never to be an old woman—but then—always to have lessons to learn! Oh, I shouldn't like that!'*
>
> —Lewis Carroll, *Alice's Adventures in Wonderland*

The death of the girl occurred in the 2000s. It might have been between the time of Carrie Bradshaw's thirty-fifth birthday (this episode first aired in the US on 3 June 2001) and the series' last episode (22 February 2004) when Carrie would have been thirty-seven.

I am of a very old generation of girls, only a little post–Carrie Bradshaw, the generation of old girls who came to writing through blogging, and onscreen journalism. Lite. My personal brand was 'trivial'.

Like many women, I came up the dirty way, writing about myself and writing about objects, aware that my image, or its reflection in the objects it handled, might at any time splash dirt. But I most fervently wished for each object to have a self and for my self to be an object among objects, having been taught from my earliest years this was desirable and that to be a desirable object was what I should desire. By telling this history of myself as an object whose objective was to desire to be an object, I may mark some difference between my self and them. But I can't help but wonder, can one object consume another?

Marie Calloway can't help but wonder about being too young. Catherine Sanderson describes herself as 'the wrong side of thirty', but her posts about her job are tagged 'working girl'.[51] In *Aliens and Anorexia*, Chris Kraus's Gudrun Sheidecker is forty-eight. And I can't help but wonder, When does girlhood end? When *SATC* ended, Carrie was not only still a girl but more a girl as each year went by, more *girl* as the word needed more and more work to bring about a fit between itself and the world. It's hard when you know some objects age better than you—clothes, housewares, shoes—that they may outlast you, especially if they remain no more than your objectives.

The girl is always too late or too soon. Guilty of bad timing, the girl is most girl when, as in *SATC*, she insists on girlhood at the exact moment it seems logically impossible. Unlike the classic tautologous logic statement 'no bachelor is married', these 'girls' are *necessarily* neither young nor virgins. Partaking simultaneously of a proposition and its negative, they exist somewhere in the excluded middle and are active in Sedgwick's 'middle ranges of agency'.

During my own stint as a young girl, I was interviewed and photographed by a French glossy magazine that took four years off my age 'for the sake of our consumer demographic'. I felt compromised, but who had made this compromise, them or me? I was temporarily a temporally flexible object. 'Girl' is an attempt to make time go backwards or sideways, and for this reason it can be very useful to write as a girl online.

Espen Aarseth defines 'cybertext' (any text that involves the reader in a 'selective movement') as 'ergodic', 'from the Greek words *ergon* and *hodos*, meaning "work" and "path"': 'nontrivial effort is required to allow the reader to traverse the text'.[52] So writing online is something to do with work and something to do with orientation. Traversing anything takes time, which the girl refuses to admit, making girl-time more trivial (less effortful, more tautologous, simultaneous, hyperlinked) and more complex. Which leads me to wonder, *Does the diary blog only seem to carve a linear temporal line through rhizomatic cyberspace?*

The girl's infinite loop could be called 'bootstrapping' or, in computing, 'booting', where a smaller program (the strap) recursively launches a larger (not only the boot but its wearer). This recursion is a form of self-reflection: 'seed AI' is a thought experiment in which an artificial intelligence is imagined to bootstrap 'recursively', to learn to teach itself to become better at self-improvement—how *singular*! Which reminds me that none of the *SATC* girls has visible origins—Miranda's mother appears only at her own funeral. They materialised in NYC fully formed, dragging themselves up recursively by the straps of their Manolos via their own invisible labour.

Reproduction, rather than repetition, doesn't get you far in this girl work. If repetition is self-similar, tautologous, I found my own reproduction made me actually nobody. Like Baby—the first computer with a memory and the progenitor of the first commercial computer, Manchester University's Ferranti Mark I—to produce offspring created not my child but my self, as a wiped disk.

'Hello, World!'

(Reproduction is the death of the girl.)

'A game—even of dolls', writes Luce Irigaray, 'is never simply active or passive but rather frustrates that opposition by the economy of repetition it puts into play . . . To play with a representation of the self. No fiction, no mimetic game, is allowed the little girl if it involves herself or her relationship to (re)production. Such games are "phallic".'[53] If the action of any rom-com ends with the girl getting the guy, the girl-diarist is on dangerous ground. Girl-time loops forever. There is no performance for what, if girlhood achieves its conventional end, comes after.

Until recently there have been few personal accounts—fictional or 'non'—that deal with the experience of motherhood.[54] Two *SATC* stars (Sarah Jessica Parker, who played Carrie, and Cynthia Nixon, who played Miranda) disguised their pregnancies while playing their roles in two different series. Sanderson's *Petite* is unusual in claiming girl status for a woman who has already reproduced. Nevertheless, 'the end of my writing experiment', Sanderson wrote in a final blog entry, 'coincided with the birth of my second child, in 2009. I no longer felt comfortable writing about my own life or borrowing from the lives of my friends'.[55]

'Hello, World!' is a beginning. At the same time, it is a test that the program is executable. It ends where it began. If the beginning of life (according to Julia Kristeva) shares abject properties with its end, I can't help but wonder if '"I" am in the process of becoming an other at the expense of my own death'.[56]

(A self-replicating machine is a thought experiment in AI: production is switched to self-reproduction.[57] But a 'useless machine' is a machine that turns itself off. It does not exist to turn anyone on, including itself. It refuses all labour including that of reproducing itself. It would prefer not to.)

Girls, writes Susan Sontag, 'are old as soon as they are no longer very young', and ageing, for girls, 'is a crisis that never exhausts itself, because the anxiety is never really used up'.[58] Berlant's 'slow death' is a related condition.[59] When 'cruel optimism' offers an impossible good life, dying becomes the material of everyday: a postponement of death when the only other option is dying quicker. IRL, this is an inevitability. It is also an endlessly fruitful narrative strategy, a musical motif that provides time for modulation, for staying with the trouble. And I can't help but wonder, Is a diary in its 'incompleteness' a murder mystery? And, If so, is it a tale told by the victim?

Or, as Derrida, who tells me that the final aporia is a pause on the border of life and death, can't help but wonder, if death is an aporia, how to properly die.[60]

Russian Doll

> *'I—I'm a little girl,' said Alice, rather doubtfully, as she remembered the number of changes she had gone through that day.*
>
> —Lewis Carroll, *Alice's Adventures in Wonderland*

I can't help but wonder, Where did I come from? How did I get here? Of what am I made? Frankenstein questions. No, not Frankenstein, the monster. They are also the questions Alice asks.

'Logic sometimes breeds monsters', wrote logician Henri Poincaré, and these monsters, like Frankenstein's, whose name is so often applied to his creation, bootstrap their progenitors: 'Formerly, when a new function was invented, it was in view of some practical end. Today they are invented on purpose to show our ancestors' reasonings at fault, and we shall never get anything more out of them.'[61]

A monster dies slowly. It is what is caught in time and what time snags on. A logical impossibility: an 'old' girl is a 'pathological' programming input that causes an algorithm to 'behave' anomalously but does not mean the algorithm fails to continue to fulfil its function. A monster of indecision, she pauses in its process of bootstrapping, unable to decide whether to run or halt.

(In subject-oriented programming, a point of view is taken on *the object. That point of view is use.)*

Carrie's bus-borne *mise en abîme*, in which she is met by her own gaze, is the equivalent of a Gödel number, or an autological sentence that proves its own unprovability as in: 'This sentence "When preceded by itself in quotes, is unprovable," when preceded by itself in quotes, is unprovable.' We are left with what cannot be decided. We are left in aporia. Our only realistic choice is ataraxia.

Here is an Alice question: *Why am I telling you this?*

(Make it personal! hisses the agent. That's what people care about!)

I confess: between 2005 and 2009, I kept a diary blog in the key of girl, though I was in no way in a girl situation: I was an (m)other. My diary told no lies and, though it was very personal, it was not about my private life, the life I was obliged to live in private, in which my labour produced the conditions that made possible other narratives that excluded me from telling mine.

I in no way laboured to make my labour of motherhood a story. I stuck to the aspects of my life that fitted the girl genre because it was, as Berlant says, 'safer to open oneself up to reiterated forms than to persons or fetishes' as 'ways of using the episodic relief of particular exchanges in order not, for a minute, to be that ordinary failed person with that history. Even if one risks self-negation through such tendencies, not to be that person is an amazing thing'.[62] Berlant was right! It was amazing to be a thing, an object, a girl. I gave myself a girl persona with all its future-forward possibility. I tripped (if not in high heels), I tried my best to experience without learning—infinite loop.

('Agent-oriented' programming is an extension of programming with 'objects'. Agents are like objects in that they consist of data plus behaviour, but they are teleological, governed by an end goal. They are double agents, used for message passing between humans and machines, passing in language as both. They are aimed at making the user's life easier when they use an app, in order to be used by it.)

An agent will be with you shortly.

When the agent arrived, she asked me to sell my blog as a novel.

('Aspect-oriented' programming can solve both these situations. Defining a use that cuts across subjects, aspects can be selected without otherwise affecting the program objects. Aspects can also modulate themselves.)

I did not.

The screen is full of speech acts.

Some of them will name a revolution that comes about.

Though there are so many of them, how can we ever know?

But:

Even if nothing happens there will have been
nothing so precious as
this real fake feeling.
or the fact it was proved true.

(Remember, proof and truth are not the same thing.)

However—

'Soyez réalistes, demandez l'impossible!'[63]
Because:

The beauty in the street throws a stone, like the girl on the 1968 poster.

She has taken to the streets in a body. She is also present as an image.
At whom does she throw the stone? At her own image? No. Outward at the viewer.

What would I ask the girl to do
if this were speculative fiction?
(Why ask her to do anything?)
Would she refuse her content
which she gives so freely?
Should she refuse her image
which is always (a) given?
How could she act without appearing?
—perhaps in text!—
Could I reboot from memory
if I could recall, for example
her symphony and song back
before self-
representation before
I was old enough to be a girl:
the image of Naomi Campbell,
her first photoshoot in Elle
magazine in WHSmith in Steven
-age in the '80s
where I went to read the magazines
but never buy them.
<She was so beautiful she caused a halt/>.

Thought Experiment #6: Sound

When do you abandon an identity online? I mean, when do you stop writing it?

Life offscreen has a strange blank quality. I listen but hear nothing.
How strange, I have always wanted
the chance to stop being.
I've always been friends with silence.
(Look how I'm shouting this!)

Silence is a sign of system failure.
Silence is also a system (Look what communicates in parentheses!
Look what data is gathered!)

On YouTube, a video of a lecture by the artist Hito Steyerl: a research engineer is breaking windows to teach AI the sound of breaking glass.[1] *'It feels strange the first time you do it,' says the engineer, whose function is not normally to break windows. 'The second time it's exciting and the third time it becomes work. That's because you have to keep doing it over and over again.'*

In 1869, Charles Baudelaire broke panes of glass, but they were not his windows. He yelled, 'Make life beautiful again!' at a man who could provide no glass that screened 'real life' with pleasant colours. Then he smashed the glazier's goods, worrying all the time only for the good of his own soul.

Baudelaire wrote about breaking windows once, but somebody's windows are always being broken. Baudelaire was smashing the windows of sentimentality that belonged to Arsène Houssaye, who had written the poem 'Le Chanson du Vitrier' about a starving glazier who could get no work because no windows were being broken. (This is a different poem again from Jacques Prevert's twentieth-century 'Chanson du Vitrier', in which the glazier is part of a system of working-class tradespeople labouring in happy reciprocity.)

By breaking the panes belonging to the glazier that—like Steyerl's engineer's glass—had never been used as windows, Baudelaire cuts out the middleman of function. Whatever: both Baudelaire and Houssaye's glaziers end up out of work.

'A thought experiment', says Steyerl, 'is cheaper and much faster' than a proof IRL. But glass only speaks when it is broken. Steyerl, running the engineers' dialogue through a Markov chain text generator, found it produced the window as a speaking subject.[2] *But still not the glazier.*

Phones recognise the sounds of their own bodies breaking, the screen that keeps their insides working. The engineers Steyerl filmed were breaking windows in order to develop private security technology to substitute for the police, producing 'a luxury version of a war zone'. Speech makes what private, public. 'Artificial stupidity', she said, 'can break every window in every street.' But 'windows', said another of the engineers, 'are a lot harder than you think . . . We are actually taking a hammer and breaking a window. So, this is reality.' 'As an artist,' says Steyerl, 'you are always being accused of being completely inconsequential and having no effect at all on the real world.'

What is the difference between poetics and poesis? Is either of them politics? Whose windows is it ok to break with art, and when?

I am talking to my friend Caroline who is an artist. We are working together on a speaking robot that is a body without organs, in collaboration with some women who are activists IRL. She will wire its body and I will write its words. The activists are its material. And we are always saying to each other,

How can we make art that has any kind of effect in the real world?

And also:

Is it enough to depict action?

Or have we been granted a residency in a place from which we can say nothing? If we speak from this place, will it immediately pay back whoever granted us this residency?

Switch off social media: dust settles on the work of self. Time to hear things IRL, accidental things. Onscreen, hearing is replaced by reading, and there's such clamour in writing. There are times when I wonder if I could backpedal on identity when my identity is so bound up with what I have written online. Is it possible to break that squared circle that is worded silence?

7
The Unwritten

The Unwritten

She was afraid that the crown might come off: but she comforted herself with the thought that there was nobody to see her.'

—Lewis Carroll, *Through the Looking-Glass*

I stopped writing online. I stopped writing blogs, I stopped writing on Facebook, I stopped writing on Instagram. Only Twitter was left, and Twitter was nothing but writing.

Then I finally deleted Twitter and saw the walls of my room, which was small and bare, without even a looking glass. Which had been more 'real'? I walked out of the room and into the street. It was empty. I could shout and no one would hear me. I could do anything, but there was nothing to do. Or there was no one to do it, including me. I had handed over the narrative to those who were still online. I had lost. I became one of the unwritten.

The Work of Mourning in the Age of Digital Reproduction

Because a work of art is always a work of mourning.

How often I've contemplated literary suicide! Not 'not to write'; I mean the excluded middle of not to publish, but leave my work as legacy. Everyone wants to bring their story to a happy end; at the same time, they want to read the obits. I have a plan: I'll let it out I'm dead a while before, that's if I have the chance. I've always had this thing about disappearing. To disappear, you have to have appeared. The screen is perfect for this; disappearing is part of the act. I am always aware of the possibility my screens might 'die', might cease to demonstrate anything: my laptop its own memento mori, or maybe mine.

'In the early days', writes one codifier of online sarcophagi, Elaine Kasket, 'Facebook simply deleted the profiles of the dead, a policy that changed as the site became such a nexus in life that its significance for death was also transformed. By 2014, Facebook representatives were using the model and language of stewardship.'[1] Deadsocial.org, an app that helps you (before death) or your loved ones (after) to manage your posthumous accounts, is at the time of writing still in beta testing.[2]

What use is death to the living? 'It is only after his death, eventually, that the writer of abjection will escape his condition of waste, reject, abject.' (Kristeva) 'Then, he [*sic*] will either sink into oblivion or attain the rank of incommensurate ideal. Death would thus be the chief curator of our imaginary museum.'[3] The Danish sociologist Michael Hviid Jacobsen, writes Kasket, 'believes that a new shift has occurred ... and that we now find ourselves in the "Age of Spectacular Death" in which the quick and the dead are continuously shuffled together on the internet like a pack of cards'.[4] DOSM (dead on social media) doesn't necessarily mean physical death, but Twitter expands the number of people you can mourn. I am still following the writer Jenny Diski's account. Though she died now some years ago, she still follows me. We met only once IRL. To me, she was near-virtual. What do you tweet to a dead person?

'Hello,
—World?!?'
(If mourning is a process, where's the processor?
Is there something reproductive about dying?)

Mostly, if you google DOSM you get articles on 'dead' sites, online death being a refusal to update. 'If grief were more consistent', writes Kasket, 'it would be better for business.'[5] The dead are not a lively consumer market. The work of mourning is neat. It is like tidying, like slenderising, like getting rid. Neatness implies the previous existence of messiness. Both are a history in objects, and any history has its objectives, stretching back in a recursive temporal narrative line, just as every object, in object-oriented programming, has its 'inheritance' that dictates its 'behaviour'. What does it mean to fetishise cleaning anyway? In the shop near me called Objects of Use there is also a section called CLEAN containing so many cleaning objects including a

computerbrushabookbrushdustbrushnumber1dustbrush
number2dustbrushnumber4(higherduster)featherdusters
1thru4blindbrushandlilydustingbrush.

I had no idea you could clean in so many different ways.

(I go with my son to the Kafka Museum in Prague. He is twelve years old. I do not usually go into writers' museums, afraid to take their objects for their subject. Kafka left almost nothing, asking his friend Max Brod to destroy his manuscripts, which we now know as his novels. Brod didn't. 'What would you do?' I ask my son. 'Destroy them', he says, 'definitely.')

A legacy may be, one day, something for a son to deal with. I read about Swedish Death Cleaning. It's like Marie Kondo but inverse. If Kondo is about self, SDC is all about the objects those left behind would like to inherit: don't keep what sparks joy in you but in your inheritors. I am already engaged in this, wanting to leave nothing behind, not even my work.

('Did you hear about that guy in the Bataclan attack in Paris? He was playing dead. A terrorist shot him in the foot to see if he was alive. But—get this!—he had a fake leg!' I am sitting with my son in the Kafka Museum in Prague. He tells me all the terrible ways people can die; I tell him all the terrible ways people can survive.)

There is no more 'moving' process than the process of mourning. It moves you without anything happening.

Writing is an act of mourning.
Writing is a speech act about what bodies can be mourned.
To read Freud's *Mourning and Melancholia* again is always an act of mourning.

The Tote Bag Theory of Fiction and the String Bag Theory of Speculative Fabulation

'That is not said right,' said the Caterpillar.

'Not quite right, I'm afraid,' said Alice, timidly; 'some of the words have got altered.'

'It is wrong from beginning to end.'

—Lewis Carroll, *Alice's Adventures in Wonderland*

'In the beginning was the deed', wrote Sigmund Freud in *Totem and Taboo*. He's clear it was murder, but he can't remember how the deed was done. He 'assumes' that 'thought passe[d] directly into action' without the need for speech acts or other mediating technologies.[6] But that was prehistory, so how could he tell? Was it a crime of telling, then, or a crime against telling?

In 'The Carrier Bag Theory of Fiction', Ursula Le Guin questions such hero narratives, linear tales, usually focused on a single man, whose storyline involves violence and power. This is the same story, she writes, that structures and reinforces the story that tells us the first tool was a knife, a spear, a club.

Le Guin did not find that these stories cast her as a subject as, for her, a knife, a spear, a club were not objects of use: 'If that's what it took, to make a weapon and kill with it, then evidently I was either extremely defective as a human being, or not human at all.' 'Wanting to be human too,' she writes, 'I sought for evidence that I was', but the hero narrative was full of holes. 'It is the story that makes the difference. It is the story that hid my humanity from me, the story the mammoth hunters told about bashing, thrusting, raping, killing, about the Hero.'[7]

Instead, Le Guin tells us that the first tool, and the shape of the first narrative, was most likely: 'A leaf a gourd a shell a net a bag a sling a sack a bottle a pot a box a container. A holder. A recipient.'[8]

When I think of Le Guin's 'Carrier Bag Theory of Fiction', I think of a string bag, a bag that looks like a net. That's what my mother shopped with, for parts of animals that she had not killed with a spear or a club but might later attack with a kitchen knife or other domestic implement. And after a long interval of plastic bags, I have a string bag now, too. A string in programming is a series of characters (it's so difficult for even programmers to avoid narrative).

Like the hero story, a single string is linear. But a net has volume, like a 3D list in programming, which is a list of 2D lists, which is a list of strings. Strings that form nets can hold things, and 'net' is a word for what can be held onto. On tinned food you see a number on the label that says 'net weight' meaning the contents without packaging, and without the water that cushions some comestibles, leaving the useful contents: a hill of beans. Is that content without form, without hierarchy or without style? Or perhaps it is content without branding.

(Now we have tote bags that retain totes everything, and also provide packaging that advertises not what is inside but usually some thing elsewhere, a speech act that hopes to bring about a fit not between world and content but between wearer and world.)

Speculative fabulation—a Donna Haraway coinage—is, like Le Guin's work, a species of 'science fiction'. It does not hope to bring about a fit between words and world but a fit between possible worlds and words. Speculative fabulation is not 'a story we tell ourselves in order to live'. Joan Didion's famous quote from *The White Album* has been cut from its context to appear on inspirational websites, but the stories that concerned Didion did not 'pay it forward' but were recursive: 'We look', she writes, 'for the sermon in the suicide', not attempting to form the future but to make sense of the past. (Interestingly, Didion says we find it 'interesting' to know.)

Eventually the 'flash pictures in varying sequence' from which Didion made her essays and journalism became 'images with no "meaning" to her beyond their temporary arrangement'.[9] Didion was alarmed by the holes she found in the narratives she tried to string together, but Haraway sees not the holes in the net but the strings: 'My multispecies storytelling is inflected through SF in all the fibres of the string figures that I try to pattern and to relay.'[10]

Strings woven form 'thick material', which makes me think of Clifford Geertz's 'thick description', which, like Akerman's *Jeanne Dielman*, accounts for hidden labour with a narrative laboured to the point of overtime.[11] Haraway notes, 'The past is the contested zone ... our thick, not-yet-fixed present, where what is yet-to-come is now at stake.'[12] Woven, text becomes texture (the words have a shared etymological root) with the addition of a final '-re', which has come to mean 'regarding' but originally meant 'from the thing', which is the ablative case of 'res', which means 'matter' in the sense of 'what matters', as in 'subject matter' or, more directly, 'matter, thing' (ok, I got that from the 'net: Online Etymology Dictionary).[13] 'Re' refers to some *thing* outside the text with which text is interwoven—something material, an object.

'The Tote Bag Theory of Fiction' brings about a fit between world and words.

'The String Bag Theory of Speculative Fabulation' puts the world into words to bring about a fit with what the world could be.

Shitstory

> *The boundary between the inner and outer is confounded by those excremental passages in which the inner effectively becomes outer, and this excreting function becomes, as it were, the model by which other forms of identity-differentiation are accomplished. In effect, this is the mode by which Others become shit.*
>
> —Judith Butler, *Gender Trouble*

My life consists of things about me that are untold. Such an effort to tell them again and again, to find the words. I could replace 'history' with 'shitstory'. Shitstory is a story that doesn't make sense, that is nonlinear, tautologous, trivial.

I'm *nibbling* into *bits* of these stories, as they are crumbs falling through the string bag theory of fiction.[14] And I have embarked on an ethics of mentioning, a repetitive function that repairs the strings of durational labour with a labour of durational art. Here is my project:

Objects

- Loudhailer
- Public space (The Spire, Dublin; Place de la République, Paris; nowhere in London as there are no more public spaces)

- Business cards with names only (one name per card): A. M. Hilton, Chantal Akerman, Marie Calloway, Catherine Sanderson, etc.
- Caroline/other working partner
- The internet

Process

- Recite the names only, through the loudhailer, passing it from one partner to the other at each name change.
- While this happens, the other partner distributes business cards matching the name to passersby. After a while, we swap tasks.
- Spend between five and fifteen minutes mentioning each name, varying tone, speed and volume of mentioning, before passing on to the next name.

Thought Experiment #7: Nothing

Writing a self online is two kinds of work.
One kind of work is the work of writing.
Another is the work that writing can do.

One thing about writing online is you can get something for nothing.
Another thing about writing online is you can get nothing for something.
Another thing about writing online is that nothing can become something.
And another thing about writing online is that something can become nothing.
The second is capitalism.
But the first is art.

Or art is also (non-exclusive OR) capitalism because, as Chris Kraus wrote, 'Art will always be transactional', and the art of the transaction is also the art.[1] *The art of the transaction is a personal art, and that art takes place between persons. It can be a very personal art because sometimes those persons are the only ones that see it.*

The problem with the screen is the same problem as the problem I had with someone who wanted me to help him rehearse to audition for the part of King Lear, a part he didn't get. He asked me to listen to his lines and one line came out blank: 'Our basest beggars / are in the poorest things superfluous.'[2] *Or to put it another way, 'I got plenty of nuttin.'*[2] *Why does it take so many words to describe what you haven't got? Anyway, he didn't get it and I couldn't ask, 'What is it about nothing you don't get?' just as Goneril and Regan couldn't bring themselves not to appear polite.*

Googling 'Poetry makes nothing happen', answers.com reminds me it is a line by W. H. Auden.[3] *Then it asks me:*

Why does nothing happen when you step on the gas?
What happens if the president does nothing to a bill?
What makes poetry different from other writings?
Does eating nothing make you fat?
What will happen if nothing is done about pollution?
Nothing will happen in 2012?
How can you make money from nothing?
What makes nothing nothing?
How can you make your friend unmad at you?[4]
How do you make dip with nothing?
What to do if your into your best friends boyfriend i wont see him again but i will be mad if nothing happens while i have the chance to make something happen?
How to make money from poetry?

Writing can be a kind of apology for power.
But there's no such thing as poverty of language.

I began to write onscreen as soon as I had enough money. In other words, when I realised I had objects, I mean material objects: enough money to convert into enough objects at a steady rate in the object economy. It's not easy to predict when enough is enough, but it's easy to feel when it happens. I had no idea that one side effect of having enough objects would be writing.

PART III
A USER MANUAL FOR ALICIAN SUBJECTS

8

'Now Would Be Good'

In these last days of being human, we find that we never were.

Just what kind of subject do they think I am? asks a pregnant friend who works with men who develop programmes for 'orienteering' cities online.

Subjectivity (still) requires I find a form.

But form eludes me.

The first citation of 'cyberculture' in the *OED* was in 1963, from Alice (A. M.) Hilton's book *Logic, Computing Machines, and Automation*. It posits the digital self as a consumer who does not work: 'In the era of cyberculture, all the ploughs pull themselves and the fried chickens fly right onto our plates.'[1]

To consume is to be accorded the right to complain (though consumption used also to be the name for a complaint). The best venue for complaint is online. It's where you're more likely to get through.

Is writing a self online a complaint because it allows me to complain?

But I do not want my writing to be made of complaint.
And I do not want my self to be made of complaint.[2]
I also don't want my self to be made of compliant.
But I can't help my self being made of writing.

If you can't complain, you might as well talk to the screen. Another Alice, 'Alicia', wrote some sad poetry about the universe in 2014 on hellopoetry.com.[3] The poetry both complains and presents as a symptom. Hello Poetry is a 'poetry community' where poets post and comment on each other's work. Alicia's work is on 'missing'. Missing is a point in space–time where what is missed is not. Because there is something there that misses, missing is some kind of evidence of self. Alicia's hashtags are #feelings #sad #depressed #alone #galaxy #universe #star #body #emotions #overthink. In order to see the comments on Alicia's poems, I would have to become a user of Hello Poetry.

(Am I having some kind of consumer experience?)

In order to become a user, I would have to submit a poem.
In order to submit a poem, I would have to submit to a culture in which poetry is a complaint.
Or what I mean is,
a user is what is used.

Only poetry keeps us here.
Only poetry will get us out of here.

'Writing is a labour of being; it needs material to work with', wrote Berlant.[4] My labour being all I possess, I have no choice but to also be that material.

Already this morning someone told me they'd pay two hundred dollars for a translation into Spanish of a short piece I don't have time to finish writing.

Instead, before 9.37 a.m. I'd assembled a piece of IKEA furniture and rejected a request for guests to stay as by that date I'd have run out of sheets. I left the washing up from breakfast in the sink with the washing up from yesterday. And I favourited a friend's tweet thread about internet ethics which was about her work—I mean her job—and also about her life.

(It's all about working out when things are working for me.
It's all about working out when I'm being worked over.)

But to use my usedness changes nothing, except for my self.

Thought Experiment #8: Test

Read the following paragraph and answer the questions:

In How to Do Things with Words, *J. L. Austin wrote that to make a speech act that declares its function is an 'explicit' performance but that to express a function privately is an 'implicit' performance. Binary information can have one of two possible states: true or false, or, less emotively, the values one or zero. Performative speech acts cannot be assigned these values as they do more than describe a state. As well as effecting change, a speech act changes affects. A performative speech act that declares functions it cannot self call, Searle called 'unhappy'. If its functions accord with its declaration, he called it 'happy'. An unhappy speech act yearns: it lies to the present but tells the truth in another dimension. It objects to what is* AND *compensates for what is not very evenly distributed yet. An unhappy declaration can be an 'error', which, declaring itself, can be corrected, or, more seriously, a 'mistake', which does not.* Happy *contains 'hap', the element of chance. It is by chance that our affective positions visit us, or perhaps by fate. 'If someone has a fate, then it's a man', writes Elfriede Jelinek in* Women as Lovers: *'If someone gets a fate, then it's a woman.'*[1]

Questions:

1. J. L. and A. M. both conceal their gender by using their initials. Whose speech act is 'happy', and whose is 'unhappy'?

2. J. L. has been declared a 'man' and A. M. a 'woman'. In concealing their given genders, is one of their performances 'implicit' and the other 'explicit'? Which?

3. If John Searle wrote in 1989 that 'the successful performance of the speech act is sufficient to bring about the fit between words and world', can A. M. = J. L. be considered a successful (happy) symmetric relation?[2]

4. If, as Bach and Harnish wrote in 1982, performatives are successful only insofar as recipients infer the intention 'implicit' in the meaning, what can be inferred from J. L. and A. M.'s respective works of self?[3]

5. If J. L. and A. M. both deprive themselves of gender, is this renaming 'transformative' (according to Kosofsky Sedgwick) in a) the purpose of the writer; XOR (exclusive or) b) the inference of the reader (according to Harnish/Bach); OR (inclusive or) c) both?

6. Can things do themselves? What kind of speech act is poetry?

7. If Judith Butler says that performativity is 'that reiterative power of discourse to produce the phenomena that it regulates and constrains', what is the illocutionary force of silence?[4]

8. In making this list of questions, what sorts of explicit and inexplicit speech acts do I commit?

9
Alice Online

(A selfie of Paris Hilton on Instagram dressed for Halloween as sexy Alice in a blue satin minidress, her pinafore morphed into a waitress's apron. She is holding a tray bearing a drink. Is it for her or is she a server?)

What's a girl to do with communication technology? I mean both 'Why is a girl like a screen?' and 'What is she doing in front of it/on it?' Why, selling herself, of course, writes McLuhan: 'The telephone, in the case of the call-girl, is like the typewriter that fuses the functions of composition and publication.'[1]

(There is another Alice who is a Hanson robot, like Sophia. She has 'frubber' [flesh-rubber] skin that looks simultaneously tactile and repellent: the so-called 'uncanny valley' of doll flesh. Unlike Turing's computer, she is not pretending to be a woman but an actress.[2] *As she is only head and shoulders, like a Girls' World styling head, her acting skills only go so far. Her lip-synch isn't great, and her face isn't super mobile. She debuted at the Rote Fabrik Theatre in Zurich in 2017, and when I see*

her perform onscreen, though she speaks German and I can't understand, I can hear that her voice is 'dramatic'—not like someone in a dramatic situation IRL but like a screen star—showing how well she can act, proving her 'femininity' via a propensity for performance, as in the Turing test. But unlike Sophia, Alice is not AI: her performance is a recording, not a live response. Alice is also, though I can't discover why, called Eva.)

'Technology in some way is always implicated in the feminine. It is young; it is thingly', writes Avital Ronell in *The Telephone Book*.[3] The question 'What is a woman?' interfaces with 'What is a screen?' McLuhan's 'call-girl'—a cyborg subject: simultaneously sex object, facilitating technology, and boundary—is an interface for getting through to . . . what? Not to a woman but to a girl online, to the interface the woman constructs, a renewable hymen spread out across nonlinear, technological time. Technologically enabled sex is both an invitation and a prophylactic: it facilitates social reproduction while screening biological generation. Hilariously incredulous that the phone's umbilical cord might be a party line for those unlikely bedfellows, the 'before' and 'after' of sex and motherhood, McLuhan notes with surprise that the 'call-girl not only lives at home, she may be a matron'.[4]

(There is an IRL Alice Eve who is also an actress but must not be mistaken for the robot. Born into a life of extraordinary privilege in terms of wealth and connections, she could have chosen almost any kind of life. Like robot Alice [Hanson], she became a screen star.)

What technology propagates is technology: 'Like the bees in the plant world, men have always been the sex organs of the technological world', wrote McLuhan.[5] 'Imagine the day', writes Derrida, 'when we will be able to send sperm by post card'—or, in the age of digital reproduction, by email or DM.[6] But who, as Derrida also asks, is the real recipient? Lacan answers, 'Might a letter on which the sender retains certain rights then not quite belong to the person to whom it is addressed? Or might it be that the latter was never the real receiver?'[7] 'Return to sender' or, to speak digitally, 'Delivery to the following recipients failed permanently.'

Women have always been at the interface of communication technology: from telephonists and telegraph operators to 'computers', the early coders whose key-tapping associations with secretarial work tagged the profession female. Sadie Plant notes how nineteenth-century telegraph offices recruited young women, 'no experience necessary'.[8] Or perhaps what was necessary was their renewable inexperience. The mother backpedals in time, existing onscreen as 'not a mother yet'.

(A piece of porn: a man and a woman playing boss and secretary. Fucked from behind over an office chair, she picks up the phone and answers—an echo on the line responding to Edison's first demand, 'Watson, I need you'—'I'm coming.')

McLuhan's telephone provides the parameters for the girl to construct what she also sells, but McLuhan calls her a call-girl not because she calls but because she comes when she is called: the girl is always on the receiving end. He misses out the caller (presumed male). Avital Ronell's *The Telephone Book* begins in media res of a call: 'We are inclined to place the telephone not so much at the origin of some reflection but as a response,' proposing that no creation myth, certainly not that of communication technology, should be first-person (masculine) singular: 'As with shoes, the telephone, or a schizophrenic, Alexander Graham Bell was not one, but a pair.'[9]

If a telephone call is somewhere between a contract and a folie à deux (Ronell says not only do we 'accept' the call but that the ear calls for it), a digital screen is content to sit in the background, what McLuhan calls a 'cool medium' inviting—no, demanding—involvement. Is there a readiness we experience in front of the screen as Heidegger does before a 'call'? The digital screen seems—better than the telephone—to fulfil Werner Hamacher's criterion that the minimal 'condition to be able to hear something as something lies in my comprehending it neither as destined for me nor as somehow oriented toward someone else'.[10]

(Then there's another Alice. She is part of a binary couple, Alice and Bob. They are a thought experiment in RSA cryptography, an encryption method for online transactions that uses a pair of keys, in which revealing the encryption key does not also reveal the corresponding key to decrypt.)

In *My Mother Was a Computer*, N. Katherine Hayles writes about Henry James's story *In the Cage*, a story of a girl in a cage, which is also the story of the cage in the girl. His heroine, a postal clerk, seeds a love message between her betters with her personal narrative, inserting herself into their romance as both tenterhooked eavesdropper and writer. Instead of paper, the lovers use the telegraph, the forerunner of the computer running on code, words encrypted into zeros and ones.

(What Alice says is a secret. She is a secretary. Bob cannot 'read' Alice's secret. Nevertheless, he can run programs on the homomorphically encrypted data, producing an encrypted output that he can't read but which Alice can decrypt with her key to the heart-shaped lock.)

James's clerk was not the real receiver (not the 'intended' receiver or a receiver who was not 'real'?), but, going one further than Lacan, forwarding messages via the telegraph line, neither did she retain the rights of the real sender.

'What forms of "responding" are ultimately available to subjects when heeding the call to respond properly?' asks Sianne Ngai.[11] She is examining Juliana Spahr's 'transcription' of the enforced vocabularies of the workplace in Spahr's poem 'LIVE', though Ngai might as well have examined the vocabularies of 'genre' novels, or telegraph—or programming—code: forms that, internalised, interfere with the subjectivity of the helpless user. James's postal clerk, inserting herself not as a subject but as an active agent in the telegraphed romance, crosses boundaries of class and gender. She does not respond properly but improperly.

(For every Alice, there is another Eve. 'Eve' is the third person in the Alice/Bob cryptology narrative. Eve is an eavesdropper, a codebreaker and a misinformer. She accesses and modifies the information, and then forwards it in order to confuse the recipient and break the code in what is called a 'man-in-the-middle' attack. Superficially

resembling Alice's message, ambiguously gendered Eve turns the meaning of what is encoded, an act that creates Eve as an active agent.)

James's postal clerk is a cryptographic Eve, greedy for connection in what Hayles calls the 'regime of [data] scarcity', so different from our contemporary digital 'dream of information'.[12] James's postal clerk's access to data was about being in the right place at the right time. The girl online floats free in digital time, which is neither measured from IRL deixis nor irrevocably tied to her offline circumstances.

Post is what comes after: a report on the event. If the email is post-but-modern, and if 'posthuman' autocorrects on my writing software to 'postman', is the 'postman' a post-girl?

An 'unreal' receiver, the post-girl might be, according to Sianne Ngai, guilty of bad timing, of claiming a glitchy agency via her labour of transcribing material and forms. This process, far from being secondary, has become the primary mode of self-declaration online, where writing is consciously borrowed, stolen, memed. Insisting on the primacy of the secondary, of genre over 'reality', the post-girl is a disruptive interface, even, and especially, for her self.

What is the message the post-girl carries, the message she also is?

10
Post-Girl Manifesto

Yes, I confess I cannot solve the internet alone. It would take a revolution.

But what kind of revolution? The demand that I make demands is so demanding, and so many revolutions have brought me little more than my own image, my appearance everywhere, my voice simultaneously nowhere. But why should shitstory fit any manifesto?

Besides a *Hacker Manifesto*, we need a user manifesto. Or maybe we don't, for who needs exhortations based on no procedural knowledge? Ok, not a manifesto or even anti-manifesto for users but a user manual for Alician subjects.

What would that look like, virtually?

What work can be done with words?

The first word is: Manifesto

→ *Manifestation* (fr) = demonstration (en)

→ *Fait à la main* (handmade)

→ Manufactured

→ (Art)ificial

→ Aesthetic

→ Vicarious
→ Virtual
→ Virtue
→ Goods
→ Objects
→ Objectives

User Manual might look like an act that is not a speech act or like speech that refuses action. It reworks the fit between word and world, and this work is its work.

It might rework work as an act of love, which might look like what love has made manually or has hand-machined, or like machine work that has been hand-polished, with or without muscular or non-muscular integrity. Its first act of love starts with paying attention to acts of attention. It will pay attention to their materiality, and to what they are like. In the attention economy, its currency will be forms of attention. It will pay attention to what is owed, including *big time!* But it will by no means have means. It will have plenty of nothing, superfluous amounts.

Its means will not have an end, which means it will not have an object. Refusing to attach objectives to objects, it will not object to being objectified. Its currency will have shifting relational values, and its relatives will be both human and nonhuman objects. It will pay attention to small useless objects of use, like a 'bone folder', a 'lawyer's pencil' or a 'Belgian stone'. It will uselessly demonstrate their use and will usefully demonstrate their use's uselessness. Its objective here will be to object.

When it demonstrates, it will use words like 'iron' and also 'clean', and these will be verbs and at the same time nouns and adjectives. It will demonstrate using all its words, which are all the words it has access to, can borrow or steal, which means all the words it also is not. It will speak mimetically from its virtual deixical situations, which will be everyplace and no place. It will have no need for a single speaking subject. Perhaps no one ever was. Neither subject nor object, it will orient itself towards agency.

It may be *like* instances of either, and it might *like* instances of both. Working across examples, it will refuse exemplarity. It will name itself by many names, but it will not self call: there will be no call for that. It would prefer not to. It will escape *identification by* via *identification with*. It will identify with what it likes. Once it has enough likes, it will become a thing. But the thing will be the liking and not the thing.

It will become a thing because it is mentioned, and anything mentioned enough becomes a thing. A mentioned thing stops being only material and becomes good material. It will reproduce by liking and by meme, acknowledging no origin however unoriginal. Refusing the primacy of biological reproduction, it will reproduce socially on social media. As it is passed around virtually, it will never pass because it will always only be like. As it passes, it will splash you, then it will pass away. When it passes away, it will become retrospective, which is also recursive. It will embed memorialising strategies that means it will take place, and that place will be in the middle, which will not be excluded. It will use the middle ranges of agency.

I can't help but wonder if it could become an agent, but it won't be a helpful agent. It will not be with you shortly: it will always be with you. It will always be dying and so slowly that its legacy will be its lifetime achievement. It will be late, so it will run in high heels. It will trip and it will halt. And when it halts, it will end with *Hello, World!* Tripping and halting will be its genre of generating genres, and one of these genres will be genre. It will make no genrifications between genres. It will generate degenerate genres that pose aporias. But it will be ok with only being kind of ok because this is kind of the only way to be, ok?

It will be a system of accountability generated from personal accounts. It will not be the personal defined in opposition to technology. It will not thank anyone, least of all goodness, that 'humans are not reducible to computational logic', and it will not say that computers are reducible to human logic.[1] Its logic gate will not be binary but autoepistemic. When it flips the switch, it will claim experience that is not only pain, and claim experience that is not only work. It will refuse any line between labour work action and any line between labour action art. It will flip the switch as a body so that every body can speak.

It will be the first true amateur work of art.

User Manual knows use is a knife that cuts both ways and that a life of labour is necessarily a life of contemplation. User Manual will not be a manifesto, or it will not be. It will not.

It is not.

<It is/>

Thought Experiment #9: Experimental Evidence of Massive-Scale Emotional Contagion through Social Networks[1]

'Emotional states can be transferred to others via emotional contagion, leading people to experience the same emotions without their awareness.'[2]

Apparently, these experiments have been done.

Acknowledgements

Many thanks to *The Happy Hypocrite* who published an early version of 'Relativity', to Sam Riviere's *If a Leaf Falls*, which published the original version of *#Theoryplushouseworktheory*, and to *Media N Journal* who published an early version of 'Thought Experiments' in the Re@ct Proceedings Special Issue.

Thank you, McKenzie Wark, Jeremy Noel-Tod, Caroline Campbell, Florence Stevens and Elliot Stevens.

Thanks especially to Clare Connors, and always to Stephen Mulraney.

Notes

Thought Experiment #1

1 'Real pain, as real as our own, would exist in virtue of the perhaps disinterested and business-like activities of these bureaucratic teams, executing their proper functions.' Daniel Dennett, 'Toward a Cognitive Theory of Consciousness', in *Brainstorms: Philosophical Essays on Mind and Psychology* (Cambridge, MA: MIT Press, 1981), p. 167.

2 'The future's already here, it's just not very evenly distributed yet.' This possibly apocryphal remark is believed to be the work of William Gibson, and was first credited to him in Scott Rosenberg, 'Virtual Reality Check, Digital Daydreams, Cyberspace Nightmares', *San Francisco Examiner,* 19 April 1992; 'Future Has Arrived', Quote Investigator, 24 January 2012, quoteinvestigator.com.

3 'By passing on each other's personal problems, the girls sympathise with one another and so on, like a chain, thus all problems and sadnesses become collective.' Margaretta D'Arcy, *Tell Them Everything* (Galway: Women's Pirate Press, 2017), p. 78.

1. Screen Goods

1 '*Monstrer* is *montrer* [to show or demonstrate].' Jacques Derrida, 'Heidegger's Hand (*Geschlecht II*)', in *Psyche: Inventions of the Other, Volume II* (California: Stanford University Press, 2008), p. 19.

2 Judith Butler, *Notes toward a Performative Theory of Assembly* (Cambridge, MA: Harvard University Press, 2015).

3 Nesrine Malik, 'She's an Icon of Sudan's Revolution. But the Woman in White Obscures Vital Truths', *Guardian*, 24 April 2019.

4 Timothy Morton, *Hyperobjects: Philosophy and Ecology after the End of the World* (Minneapolis: University of Minnesota Press, 2013), p. 14.

5 Jacques Derrida, 'Signature Event Context', in *Limited, Inc.* (Evanston: Northwestern University Press, 1988), p. 12.

6 Aristotle, *The Nichomachean Ethics, Book 1* (Oxford: Oxford University Press, 2009), p. 3.

7 Sara Ahmed, 'Happy Objects' in *The Affect Theory Reader*, ed. Melissa Gregg and Gregory J. Seigworth (Durham, NC: Duke University Press, 2010); Judith Butler, 'Against Proper Objects', *Differences* 6, no. 2/3 (1994): pp. 1–26.

8 Fumio Sasaki, *Goodbye, Things: On Minimalist Living* (London: Penguin, 2017).

9 Claude Levi-Strauss, *Totemism* (London: Merlin Press, 1964), p. 89.

10 Fredric Jameson, *Postmodernism: Or, The Cultural Logic of Late Capitalism* (London: Verso, 1992), p. 26.

11 'Now, here, you see, it takes all the running you can do, to keep in the same place. If you want to get somewhere else, you must run at least twice as fast as that!' The Red Queen in Lewis Carroll, *Through the Looking-Glass and What Alice Found There*, chapter 2 (New York: Taylor & Francis, 2002), p. 161.

2. Relativity

1 Zero is a 'neutral number' (neither negative nor positive). It is also a 'natural number'.
2 'If each one of these toys took 600 hours to make then that's 600 hours of love; and if I gave this to you, you owe me 600 hours of love; and that's a lot. And if you can't pay it back right away, [the interest] keeps accumulating . . . That's more love than you could ever pay back. So what? You're just fucked then.' Mike Kelley, Interview, *Bomb Magazine*, January 1992, bombmagazine.org.
3 Jameson, *Postmodernism*, p. 137.
4 'In Old High German, besides "gift", the meaning also included "a dose of medicine given", whence "a dose of poison given", which finally yielded "poison"; all this probably by analogy with the Latin word *dōs* (gen. *dōtis*), which also had the meanings "gift" and "poison".' Friedrich Kluge, *Etymologisches Wörterbuch der deutschen Sprache*, 24th ed. (Berlin: De Gruyter, 2002), p. 357. The older sense 'gift' is still preserved in German in the word *Mitgift*, 'dowry', literally 'with-gift', that is, assets given to a bride by her parents on marriage (*given* to go *with* her into the new household). 'Why Does "Gift" Mean Poison in German and Present in English? Is It a Coincidence or Do They Have the Same Etymology?', Quora, quora.com.
5 Adapted from 'Is an antisymmetric and asymmetric relation the same? Are irreflexive and anti-reflexive the same', math.stackexchange.com, 2 May 2014.
6 Brian Massumi, *The Politics of Everyday Fear* (Minneapolis: University of Minnesota Press, 1993), p. ix.
7 'The saturation of the social space by fear. Have fear-producing mechanisms become so pervasive and invasive that we can no longer separate ourselves from our fear? If they have, is fear still fundamentally an emotion, a personal experience, or is it part of what constitutes the collective ground of possible experience? Is it primarily a subjective content or part of the very process of subject formation?' Ibid.
8 A. M. Turing, 'Computing Machinery and Intelligence', *Mind* 59, 236 (October 1950): pp. 433–60.

Thought Experiment #3

1 'It is interesting to note that machines designed for the use of the individual (for example, machines to provide household assistance, such as vacuum cleaners) come very late in the industrial development of society since they replace the most poorly paid workers.' A. M. Hilton, *Logic, Computing Machines, and Automation* (London: Cleaver-Hume Press, 1963), p. 370.

3. Work

1 Judith Butler, *Gender Trouble,* (New York: Routledge, 2006), p. 106.
2 Kristeva, *The Powers, of Horror: An Essay on Abjection* (New York: Columbia University Press, 1982), p. 64.
3 Butler, *Gender Trouble*, p. 80.
4 'If the mother is the original desire, and that may well be true for a wide range of late capitalist household dwellers, then that is a desire both produced and prohibited within the terms of that cultural context.' Ibid., p. 97.
5 Ibid., p. 88.
6 'For Kristeva, the semiotic expresses that original libidinal multiplicity within the very terms of culture, more precisely, within poetic language in which multiple meanings and semantic non-closure prevail. In effect, poetic language is the recovery of the maternal body within the terms of language, one that has the potential to disrupt, subvert, and displace the paternal law.' Ibid., pp. 101–2.
7 Merritt Baer, 'Can Your Robot Love You?', *Daily Beast*, 31 January 2017, thedailybeast.com.
8 Monique Wittig, 'One Is Not Born a Woman' in *Feminist Theory Reader*, ed. Carole R. McCann and Seung-Kyung Kim (London: Routledge, 2016), p. 284.
9 Marie Kondo, *The Life-Changing Magic of Tidying Up: The Japanese Art of Decluttering and Organizing* (New York: Ten Speed Press, 2014).

10 Hannah Arendt, 'Labour, Work, Action', in *The Human Condition* (Chicago: University of Chicago Press, 2018), p. 167.
11 Chosil Kil, *You Owe Me Big Time*, 2012, vimeo.com.
12 'A life without speech and without action, on the other hand . . . has ceased to be a human life because it is no longer lived among men.' Arendt, *The Human Condition*, p. 176.
13 Kristeva, *The Powers of Horror*, p. 123.
14 'Moira' of naturalreaders.com reads Butler's chapter heading '1. The Bodily Politics of Julia Kristeva' as 'I, the Bodily Politics of Julia Kristeva'.
15 This takes between two and three years.
16 'We are left with the old definition of dirt as matter out of place.' Mary Douglas, *Purity and Danger: An Analysis of Concepts of Pollution and Taboo* (Abingdon: Routledge, 2002), p. 44.
17 Lauren Berlant, 'On the Inconvenience of Other People', Jack Halberstam, 'Jack Halberstam on Queer Failure, Silly Archives and the Wild', interview at Summer School for Sexualities, Cultures and Politics, Belgrade, August 2014, 'IPAK Centar', youtube.com; Donna Haraway, 'Staying with the Trouble: Becoming Worldly with Companion Species', keynote speech at the Women's Studies Program Fifth Annual Feminist Theory Workshop, Duke University, Durham, NC, March 2011, 'DukeWomenStudies', youtube.com.
18 Jonathan Rée, 'Wittgenstein's Collection of Nonsense', 13 February 2013, iai.tv.
19 Rosi Braidotti, 'Are "We" in This Together?', 21 September 2017, YouTube.
20 John David Ebert, 'Derrida's *Of Grammatology* Part 1 by John David Ebert 1/2', 28 July 2012, YouTube.
21 Angela Nagle, at Virtual Futures, soundcloud.com, 3 July 2018.
22 McKenzie Wark, '*A Hacker Manifesto* @ MaMa', 20 March 2006, Zagreb, 'pmilat', YouTube.
23 In June 2020, I found this story had been removed from Keston Sutherland's Wikipedia page.

Thought Experiment #4

1 From the 'classical Latin *manū*, ablative singular of *manus*, hand'. 'Manufactured', *Oxford English Dictionary*, oed.com.

2 A. M. Hilton, *Logic, Computing Machines, and Automation*, p. 374.

4. Not Working

1 Martin Heidegger, 'The Question Concerning Technology', in *Basic Writings* (New York: HarperCollins, 1993).

2 Marshall McLuhan, *Understanding Media: The Extensions of Man* (Abingdon: Routledge, 2004), p. 9.

3 Ibid., p. 39.

4 Ibid., p. 99.

5 Virginia Woolf, *To the Lighthouse* (Oxford: Oxford University Press, 2008), p. 22.

6 Ibid.

7 'She asked him what his father's books were about. "Subject and object and the nature of reality," Andrew had said.' Ibid.

8 'We can talk about being wilful subjects, feminist killjoys, angry black women; we can claim those figures back; we can talk about those conversations we have had at dinner tables or in seminars or meetings.' Sara Ahmed, 'Feminist Killjoys (and Other Wilful Subjects)', *Polyphonic Feminisms: Acting in Concert* 8, no. 3 (summer 2010).

5. Am I Those Names?

1 Gertrude Stein, 'Poetry and Grammar', in *Modern Essays on Writing and Style* (New York: Holt, Rinehart and Winston, 1969), p. 71.

2 Silvia Federici, *Wages against Housework* (1974), caringlabor.wordpress.com, p. 2.

3 'The reading of "performativity" as wilful and arbitrary choice misses the point that the historicity of discourse and, in particular, the historicity of norms (the "chains" of iteration invoked and dissimulated in the imperative utterance) constitute the power of discourse to enact what it names.' Butler, *Gender Trouble*, p. 187.
4 John Searle, 'How Performatives Work', *Linguistics and Philosophy* vol. 12, no. 5, (October 1989), p. 547.
5 The descriptivist theory of proper names states that a subject can be represented by a name that links to a number of tags, for example: X is a woman; X is a girl; X is a mother. (X, having no existence online outside various 'descriptions' of her, can be said to be an identity relying on 'metalinguistic' naming.) But the appellation 'friend', which does not link to a proper name, can describe and be borrowed by anyone approaching the door. Descriptivist naming could be said to be anti-essentialist and based on function, but it can also be based in using (objectifying).
6 J. R. R. Tolkein, *The Lord of the Rings* (Boston: Houghton Mifflin, 2004), p. 306.
7 List of fake users, 'kojoney/fake_users', Github, 30 March 2013.
8 Derrida, 'Signature Event Context', p. 315.
9 'We need a name for the new replicator, a noun that conveys the idea of a unit of cultural transmission, or a unit of imitation. "*Mimeme*" comes from a suitable Greek root, but I want a monosyllable that sounds a bit like "gene". I hope my classicist friends will forgive me if I abbreviate *mimeme* to meme. If it is any consolation, it could alternatively be thought of as being related to "memory", or to the French word *même*. It should be pronounced to rhyme with "cream".' Richard Dawkins, *The Selfish Gene: Fortieth Anniversary Edition* (Oxford: Oxford Landmark Science, 2016), p. 249.
10 'Big contradictions in the evolution theory', christianforums.com, 10 August 2005, accessed 7 November 2017.
11 Ibid.
12 'Secondly, as utterances our performances are also heir to certain other kinds of ill, which infect all utterances. And these likewise, though again they might be brought into a more general account,

we are deliberately at present excluding. I mean, for example, the following: a performative utterance will, for example, be in a peculiar way hollow or void if said by an actor on the stage, or if introduced in a poem, or spoken in soliloquy. This applies in a similar manner to any and every utterance—a sea-change in special circumstances. Language in such circumstances is in special ways—intelligibly—used not seriously, but in many ways parasitic upon its normal use—ways which fall under the doctrine of the etiolations of language. All this we are excluding from consideration. Our performative utterances, felicitous or not, are to be understood as issued in ordinary circumstances.' J. L. Austin, *How to Do Things with Words* (Cambridge, MA: Harvard University Press, 1975), pp. 21–2.

13 Judith Butler, 'When Gesture Becomes Event', in *Inter Views in Performance Philosophy: Crossings and Conversations*, Anna Street, Julien Alliot, Magnolia Pauke, eds (London: Palgrave Macmillan, 2017), p. 173.

6. Girl Online

1 Avital Ronell, *The Telephone Book: Technology, Schizophrenia, Electric Speech*, revised ed. (Lincoln, NE: University of Nebraska Press, 1989), p. 141.

2 Marie Calloway, *What Purpose Did I Serve in Your Life?* (New York: Tyrant Books, 2013), p. 87.

3 Emily Gould, 'Our Graffiti', *Emily Magazine*, 29 November 2011, emilymagazine.com.

4 Eve Kosofsky Sedgwick, *Epistemology of the Closet* (Berkeley: University of California Press, 1990), p. 25.

5 'Darren Star', Wikipedia, en.wikipedia.org, accessed 27 October 2021.

6 Turing, 'Computing, Machinery and Intelligence', p. 346.

7 Rae Armantrout, *The Pretext* (Los Angeles: Green Integer, 2001), p. 9.

8 Eve Kosofsky Sedgwick, *A Dialogue on Love* (Boston: Beacon Press, 2000), p. 77.

9 Sophie Hirsch, '*Sex and the City*'s Opening Credits Almost

Looked Very Different', *W Magazine*, 30 March 2017, wmagazine.com, accessed 30 April 2019. Note this was published in the 'nostalgia' section.

10 Neha Sharma, 'Everything Carrie Ever Wondered About on Sex and the City', *Vulture*, 13 March 2013, vulture.com.

11 Marissa Blanchard, 'Darren Star Reflects Back on *Sex and the City*', HBO, no date, hbo.com.

12 'For I know not any greater blessing to a young man who is beginning life than a virtuous lover or to the lover than a beloved youth.' Plato, 'Symposium', in *The Portable Plato* (London: Penguin, 1977), p. 130.

13 'The Love who is the offspring of the common Aphrodite is essentially common, and has no discrimination, being such as the meaner sort of men feel, and is apt to be of women as well as of youths, and is of the body rather than of the soul—the most foolish beings are the objects of this love which desires only to gain an end, but never thinks of accomplishing the end nobly, and therefore does good and evil quite indiscriminately. The goddess who is his mother is far younger than the other, and she was born of the union of the male and female, and partakes of both.' Ibid., p. 133.

14 'The desire of the healthy is one, and the desire of the diseased is another.' Ibid., p. 139.

15 'The sexes were not two as they are now, but originally three in number; there was man, woman, and the union of the two, having a name corresponding to this double nature, which had once a real existence, but is now lost, and the word "Androgynous" is only preserved as a term of reproach.' Ibid., pp. 143–4.

16 'The true order of going, or being led by another, to the things of love, is to begin from the beauties of earth and mount upwards for the sake of that other beauty, using these as steps only, and from one going on to two, and from two to all fair forms, and from fair forms to fair practices, and from fair practices to fair notions, until from fair notions he arrives at the notion of absolute beauty.' Ibid., p. 171.

17 'See you how fond he is of the fair? He is always with them and

is always being smitten by them, and then again he knows nothing and is ignorant of all thing such is the appearance.' Ibid., p. 178.

18 Plato, *Protagoras and Meno* (London: Penguin Classics, 1974), p. 127.

19 Sara Ahmed, *The Promise of Happiness* (Durham, NC: Duke University Press, 2010), p. 68.

20 Lauren Berlant, *Cruel Optimism* (Durham, NC: Duke University Press, 2011), p. 20.

21 Eve Kosofsky Sedgwick, *Touching Feeling: Affect, Pedagogy, Performativity* (Durham, NC: Duke University Press, 2003), p. 13.

22 Chris Kraus, *I Love Dick* (Pasadena: Semiotext(e), 1997), p. 72.

23 User reviews of Catherine Sanderson's *Petite Anglaise* (London: Penguin, 2009), Amazon.

24 'To be affected by something is to evaluate that thing.' Ahmed, *The Promise of Happiness*, p. 23.

25 Jacques Derrida, 'The Law of Genre', *Critical Inquiry* 7, no. 1, 'On Narrative' (1980): p. 65.

26 McLuhan, *Understanding Media*, pp. 19, 221.

27 Laura Bennett, 'The First-Person Industrial Complex', *Slate*, 14 September 2015, slate.com.

28 An aphorism ascribed to Mae West, Margot Asquith and others: girl as communal identity.

29 The *New York Times* used the word 'non-writer' to describe Emma McLaughlin and Nicola Kraus, who used their real-life experience as nannies to New York's super rich to write the blockbuster *Nanny Diaries* (St. Martin's Press, 2002). Like Sanderson's, their claim that their experiences were 'real' both boosted their marketability and exposed them to criticism, personally, morally and as authors. 'It is not that a few people out there aren't hoping that *Citizen Girl* [their second book] tanks', wrote Alex Williams. 'The same image that had made them easy to market in the first place—they're not writers, they're nannies—made them easy targets.' Alex Williams, 'The Post-Nanny Diaries', *New York Times*, 21 November 2004. That their 'real' identity was associated with the particularly 'girl'-ish profession of care work (as such, opposed to the 'intellectual' work of writing) made this

targeting easier. In truth, not only were they 'non-writers'; they were non-nannies: themselves upper-middle-class white university students whose temporary positions as carers meant that their story could be easily digested by a conservative publishing and film industry without raising political issues around race or class. Their avatar, 'Nan', is also a student, providing an escape fantasy for main-job careworker-readers (as one Amazon UK reviewer puts it, the book, although about work, is 'a nice break from work or from everyday duties'). Interestingly, Williams's article was published not in the Books but in the Fashion section of the *New York Times*. *Sex and the City*, season five, episode five, author's transcription.

30 Armistead Maupin, *More Tales of the City* (London: Black Swan, 1989), p. 161.
31 Heidegger, *Poetry, Language, Thought*, (New York: Perennial Modern Classics, 2001), p. 28.
32 Berlant, *Cruel Optimism*, p. 1.
33 'What distinguishes the most flimsy pair of shoes from mere consumer goods is that they do not spoil if I don't wear them, they are objects and therefore possess a certain "objective" independence of their own, however modest. Used or unused they will remain in the world for a certain while unless they are wantonly destroyed.' Hannah Arendt, 'Labour, Work, Action', in *The Human Condition*, p. 138.
34 Berlant, *Cruel Optimism*, p. 45.
35 Ibid.
36 Luis Estrada-González, 'Models of Possibilism and Trivialism', in *Logic and Logical Philosophy, Vol. 21* (2005): p. 193.
37 Berlant, *Cruel Optimism*, p. 176.
38 T. W. Adorno, Bob Hullot-Kentor, Frederic Will, 'The Essay as Form', *in New German Critique*, No. 32 (Spring– Summer 1984), pp. 151–71, p. 153.
39 Butler, *Gender Trouble*, p. 51.
40 Chris Kraus, *I Love Dick*, p. 135; Audrey Wollen, 'Artist Audrey Wollen on the Power of Sadness', interview, *Nylon*, no date, nylon.com; Joanna Walsh, '*I Love Dick* by Chris Kraus – A Cult Feminist Classic Makes Its UK Debut', *Guardian*, 11 November 2015, theguardian.com.

41 Chris Kraus, *Aliens and Anorexia* (London: Tuskar Rock, 2018), p. 29.
42 Vahni Capildeo, 'Vahni Capildeo', *Scottish Poetry Library Podcast*, 26 January 2017, scottishpoetrylibrary.org.uk.
43 Heinz von Foerster, *Observing Systems* (Seaside: Intersystems Publications, 1984).
44 Berlant, *Cruel Optimism*, pp. 127, 128; Michel Foucault, *History of Sexuality, Vol. 1* (New York: Vintage Books, 1990), p. 58.
45 Judith Butler, 'Gender Trouble', in *Continental Feminism Reader* (Oxford: Rowman & Littlefield, 2003), p. 42.
46 Ibid., p. 180.
47 Ibid., p. 15.
48 Catherine Sanderson, 'Name Calling', *Petite Anglaise* blog, 23 August 2005, petiteanglaise.com.
49 Catherine Sanderson, 'Postscript', 1 November 2013, petiteanglaise.com.
50 Ibid.
51 Catherine Sanderson, 'Name Calling', *Petite Anglaise* blog.
52 Espen J. Aarseth, *Cybertext* (John Hopkins University Press, 1997), p. 1.
53 Luce Irigaray, *Speculum of the Other Woman* (Ithaca: Cornell University Press, 1985), p. 77.
54 The range of contemporary writing addressing motherhood, that play out as durational projects and that have influenced this work could include Jenny Offil's *Dept. of Speculation* (New York: Vintage, 2014); Maggie Nelson's *The Argonauts* (Minneapolis: Graywolf Press, 2015); Rita Galchen's *Little Labours* (New York: New directions, 2016); Sarah Manguso's *Ongoingness* (Minneapolis: Graywolf Press, 2016); Kate Zambreno's *The Appendix Project* (Pasadena: Semiotext(e), 2019); Sheila Heti's *Motherhood* (New York: Henry Holt and Company, 2019); Lauren Elkin's forthcoming *Art Monsters* (London: Chatto & Windus, 2023), and perhaps this book.
55 Sanderson, 'Postscript', *Petite Anglaise* blog.
56 Kristeva, *The Powers of Horror*, p. 3.
57 The 'RepRap' prototyped at the University of Bath in 2005 can produce some of its own components. Adrian Bowyer, 'First reprapped circuit', *RepRap: Blog*, 19 April 2009, blog.reprap.org.

58 Sontag, 'The Double Standard of Ageing', *Saturday Review*, 23 September 1972.

59 'Through the space opened by slow death, then, I seek to recast some taxonomies of causality, subjectivity, and life-making embedded in normative notions of agency. More particularly, I suggest that to counter the moral science of biopolitics, which links the political administration of life to a melodrama of the care of the monadic self, we need to think about agency and personhood not only in inflated terms but also as an activity exercised within spaces of ordinariness that does not always or even usually follow the literalizing logic of visible effectuality, bourgeois dramatics, and lifelong accumulation or self-fashioning.' Berlant, *Cruel Optimism*, p. 99.

60 'In everyday German, *verenden* also means to die, to succumb, to kick the bucket, but since that is clearly not what Heidegger means by properly dying (*eigentlich sterben*), by the dying proper to Dasein, verenden must therefore not be translated by "dying" in order to respect what Heidegger intends to convey.' Jacques Derrida, *Aporias: Dying—Awaiting (One Another at) the 'Limits of Truth'* (Stanford: Stanford University Press, 1993), p. 31.

61 Henri Poincaré, *Science and Method* (London: Thomas Nelson and Sons, 1908), p. 125.

62 Berlant, *Cruel Optimism*, pp. 139, 134.

63 'Mascolo raconte comment l'un des plus fameux slogans de Mai, "Soyez réalistes / Demandez l'impossible", vit le jour à l'écoute d'une discussion à l'usine Renault de Billancourt.' Christophe Bident, *Maurice Blanchot: partenaire invisible : essai biographique* (Ceyzérieu: Éditions Champ Vallon, 1998), p. 473.

Thought Experiment #6

1 Hito Steyerl, 'Language of Broken Glass', at Haus der Kulturen der Welt, Berlin, 12 January 2019, hkw.de.

2 A Markov generator tells you the probability of future outcomes based on knowledge of a previous event, for example, predictive

text. A Markov generator uses probabilistic logic, assigning probabilities in such a way as to maximise entropy.

7. The Unwritten

1 Elaine Kasket, 'Posthumous Posts', *Times Literary Supplement*, 29 May 2019.
2 MyWishes, mywishes.co.uk.
3 Kristeva, *The Powers of Horror*, p. 16.
4 Elaine Kasket, 'Posthumous Posts'.
5 Ibid.
6 Sigmund Freud, *Totem and Taboo* (Abingdon: Routledge, 2001), p. 187.
7 Ursula K. Le Guin, 'The Carrier Bag Theory of Fiction', in *Dancing at the Edge of the World: Thoughts on Words, Women, Places* (London: Paladin, 1989), p. 167.
8 Ibid., p. 166.
9 Joan Didion, *The White Album* (London: Fourth Estate, 2017), p. 11.
10 Donna Haraway, 'SF: Science Fiction, Speculative Fabulation, String Figures, So Far', *Ada: A Journal of Gender, New Media, and Technology*, no. 3 (2013).
11 Clifford Geertz, 'Thick Description: Toward an Interpretive Theory of Culture', in *The Interpretation of Cultures: Selected Essays* (New York: Basic Books, 1973), pp. 3–30.
12 Haraway, 'SF: Science Fiction, Speculative Fabulation, String Figures, So Far'.
13 'Re', Online Etymology Dictionary, etymonline.com.
14 In programming, a nibble is four bits.

Thought Experiment #7

1 Chris Kraus, *Social Practices*, (Los Angeles: Semiotext(e), 2019), p. 11.

2 William Shakespeare, *King Lear* (London: The Arden Shakespeare, 1997), p. 255.
3 W. H. Auden, 'In Memory of W. B. Yeats' in *Auden: Poems* (London: Everyman, 1995), p. 78; 'What was the poetry makes nothing happen?', answers.com, 2009.
4 'Talk to her tell her that i am sorry for whatever i did if she says nothing back she is not a true friend', answers.com.

8. 'Now Would Be Good'

1 Hilton, *Logic, Computing Machines, and Automation*, p. xvi.
2 I have a nominative doppelgänger on Twitter whose tweets are almost always customer complaints, for example, jo_walsh1980: '@Primark Visited the London Oxford St branch& was impressed by the new nail bar, but not with the woman who worked there. After ignoring me she finally looked up from her phone. I asked a simple question if they had OPI nail polish she said no then dismissed me by saying bye #rude', Twitter.
3 'Alicia', Hello Poetry, hellopoetry.com.
4 Lauren Berlant and Kathleen Stewart, *The Hundreds* (Durham, NC: Duke University Press, 2018), p. 58.

Thought Experiment #8

1 Elfriede Jelinek, *Women as Lovers* (London: Serpent's Tail, 1994), p. 3.
2 John Searle, 'How Performatives Work', p. 547.
3 K. Bach and R. M. Harnish, 'Linguistic Communication and Speech Acts', *The Philosophical Review* 91, no. 1 (1982): pp. 134–8.
4 Judith Butler, *Bodies That Matter: On the Discursive Limits of 'Sex'* (Abingdon: Routledge, 2011), p. xii.

9. Alice Online

1 McLuhan, *Understanding Media*, p. 290.
2 I have met only one 'male' robot in the course of my research. 'He' is 'Stevie' at Trinity College Dublin's research labs. Stevie is not AI but he is a care robot, designed as a companion and helper to enable elderly humans to live independently for longer.
3 Ronell, *The Telephone Book*, p. 207.
4 McLuhan, *Understanding Media*, p. 290.
5 Ibid. p. 239.
6 Jacques Derrida, *The Postcard* (Chicago: University of Chicago Press, 1987), p. 24.
7 Jacques Lacan, 'Seminar on The Purloined Letter', in *Essential Papers on Literature and Psychoanalysis* (New York: New York University Press, 1993), p. 284.
8 Sadie Plant, *Zeros and Ones* (London: Fourth Estate, 1998), p. 117.
9 Ronell, The Telephone Book, pp. 3, 227.
10 Werner Hamacher, 'Interventions', *Qui Parle: Journal of Literary Studies* 1, no. 2 (1987): p. 38.
11 Sianne Ngai, 'Bad Timing (A Sequel): Paranoia, Feminism, and Poetry', *differences: A Journal of Feminist Cultural Studies* 12, no. 2 (2001), pp. 1–46.
12 N. Katherine Hayles, *My Mother Was a Computer: Digital Subjects and Literary Texts* (Chicago: University of Chicago Press, 2005), p. 62.

10. Post-Girl Manifesto

1 Geoff Cox and Alex McLean, *Speaking Code: Coding as Aesthetic and Political Expression* (Cambridge, MA: MIT Press, 2012), p. 105.

Thought Experiment #9

1 A. D. I. Kramer, J. E. Guillory and J. T. Hancock, 'Experimental Evidence of Massive-Scale Emotional Contagion through Social Networks', *PNAS* 111 (2014): p. 8788.

2 Ibid.